Adolescent Suicide

A School-Based

Approach

to Assessment

& Intervention

WILLIAM G. KIRK

Research Press
2612 North Mattis Avenue
Champaign, Illinois 61821

Cover design by Doug Burnett
Composition by Graphic Sciences Corporation
Printed by McNaughton & Gunn

ISBN 0-87822-336-3
Library of Congress Catalog No. 93-84471

To Knox and Genevieve,
Jerry and Luella,
the inspiration in my life.
To Sara, Garrett, Jonathon, and Molly,
the joy in my life.
To Linda,
the love of my life.

Contents

Figures and Tables

FIGURES

TABLES

Foreword

The death of a child is the greatest challenge a parent and family can face. A self-inflicted death leaves parents, siblings, peers, educators, and mental health professionals searching to answer the question why and desperately wishing they could turn back the clock to alter the course of events. Time cannot be recaptured. However, when children and youth are nurtured and served by individuals who are sensitive to signs of distress and skilled in intervening appropriately, then the course of events can be changed before tragedy occurs. This book, appropriate for beginning and advanced professionals alike, schools each of us in the sensitivity required for accurate identification of potentially suicidal adolescents and in the skills necessary to implement effective interventions. In its pages, Bill Kirk shares his years of experience as a professional, his skills as a teacher, his objectivity as a researcher, and his compassion as a parent.

As he points out, the children and youth of today are exposed to many life stressors. However, there is little evidence that these young people are equipped to deal effectively with this stress. Growing up in America is becoming an increasingly difficult (even dangerous) task, and many adolescents are seeing few if any solutions to the problems they face.

When confronted with problems, some young people and their families seek assistance through mental health centers, guidance clinics, and private mental health practitioners. However, many youths are not so fortunate, and it is this group the schools are in a unique position to serve. With the exception of the family, school is the place in our society where adults are best able to scrutinize the behavior of young people. However, do most school professionals know how to recognize the signs of distress and what to do when they see these signs? The number of crisis teams in schools and community mental health centers has increased significantly; however, individuals other than crisis team members usually are unskilled in identifying and intervening with suicidal adolescents. All educators, counselors, school psychologists, social workers, and other mental health workers in school as well as community settings must be skilled in recognizing the signs of a potential suicide and in implementing appropriate interventions.

If we imagine ourselves the parent of an adolescent at risk for suicide, the critical nature of this need becomes clearer. As a parent, each of us trusts that the educators and mental health professionals responsible for our child will have the best training and skills available to recognize the signs of potential suicide and to deal with suicide risk once recognized. As a professional, each of us should seek the level of skill we would want a person responsible for our own child to have. Anything less is unacceptable. The information presented in this book contributes significantly toward our achievement of that important goal.

George M. Batsche
School Psychology Program, University of South Florida, Tampa
Past President, National Association of School Psychologists

Acknowledgments

A number of individuals and groups have been instrumental in helping me with this project by sharing their expertise and support. I wish to single out a few of them.

Drs. Glen Walter and Bob Saltmarsh provided unconditional support and inspiration—important in any growth experience. Dr. Mark Shatz, friend and student-turned-teacher, provided helpful and valuable suggestions during the various stages of this work. My clinical consultant, Dr. Genie Lenihan, was always there during critical moments of doubt. Pam Gutowski was exceptionally helpful in the preparation of the manuscript, and Dr. Fred Yaffe has consistently been a critical supporter of this endeavor. Diane Pence read early versions and supplied keen and professional critiques. Drs. Jerry Sattler and John Best, successful authors in their own right, provided insightful and practical suggestions. Dr. George Batsche supplied his usual enthusiasm, flexibility, and encouragement. I am grateful to them all.

The guidance department at Charleston High School, Charleston, Illinois, helped more than they know. Dolly McFarland and Mary Kay Smitley helped to remind me that the day-to-day clinical trench work is exhausting, but also every now and then, life saving.

The original research for this work began at University College, Cork, Ireland, where many friends, particularly Dr. Eleanor O'Leary, provided a stimulating and creative backdrop.

I developed many important insights into the world of the dysfunctional adolescent during consultations with the staff at the Central East Alcohol and Drug Council. Weekly meetings with the adolescent treatment team helped reinforce my interests, tested my expertise, and, more importantly, demonstrated to me how intense professionalism and commitment can help addicted and suicidal adolescents in the painstaking process toward recovery.

A very special thanks goes to the many clinicians, counselors, clients, students, teachers, administrators, and parents who willingly provided material for the case studies. The inclusion of these concrete examples in the text helped significantly in communicating the reality of adolescent pain and suicide. My insights into the struggles of survivors of suicide were increased by my participation in the Suicide Survivors Support Group of the Hospice of Lincolnland. It is difficult to express how grateful I am to the members of that group for allowing me the privilege of sharing the pain in their lives and the strength of their survivorship. The memories of Robert, Brent, Jonathan, Tom, Cindy, Randy, and Randall will live on.

My wife, Linda, and our adolescent children Sara, Garrett, Jonathon, and Molly model vitality, compassion for others, humor, and a commitment to life that I will always appreciate.

Finally, this document has been transformed from a bulky, rambling manuscript into a readable and fluid work with the professional guidance of Amita Kachru and Karen Steiner of Research Press. Their gentle persistence became a critical ingredient in the finished product. I am very grateful to them both.

Nothing seems so tragic to one who
is old as the death of someone
who is young and this proves that
life is a good thing.

—Zoe Akins, *The Portrait*

Introduction

This book is designed to assist educators, counselors, and all other caregivers who labor on behalf of young people. It is the outcome of many hours spent in counseling pained adolescents, many hours consulting with teachers and providing inservice education to concerned—sometimes frightened—school personnel, and many agonizing moments with relatives who have continually asked the question why. Throughout this process I've gained much more than I can possibly give. However, I can hope that this book helps to fill a void in the literature on adolescent suicide.

The discussion presented here is based on certain assumptions. First, knowledgeable intervention is the key to remediating the problem of adolescent suicide, reportedly our nation's number two killer of young people (Frazier, 1989). Second, educators and helping professionals need specific skills and information to assess suicide potential accurately and to intervene appropriately.

Having accurate information involves first refuting the following myths about suicide.

Young people who talk about suicide are not serious about it. This misconception has kept people from looking beyond what they might consider manipulative or attention-getting behavior. In fact, the majority of people who kill themselves, both young and old, provide a variety of clues about what they are feeling and what they are planning to do. When a young person makes statements related to death, dying, or escape, or behaves in ways that indicate preparation for death, he or she should always be taken seriously. Many deaths could be prevented if friends, relatives, or educators took these signals seriously.

A young person must be crazy to commit suicide. Although some adolescents attempt and complete suicide as a result of a psychotic condition, the majority are not mentally ill in a traditional sense at the time of death. The conclusions of many psychological autopsies, or procedures that attempt to determine the reasons for a suicide, suggest that most young people are relatively rational and coherent at the

1

time of their demise. Accepting this myth prevents people from perceiving suicide as the potential threat to all adolescents that it is.

If an adolescent wants to commit suicide, there is nothing anyone can do to prevent it. This is one of the more dangerous misconceptions because it implies that suicidal thinking is irreversible. The critical task in preventing adolescent suicide is to communicate the unacceptability of the act and to provide time for the adolescent to explore options with the support and compassion of others.

Because adolescent girls survive more frequent suicide attempts than boys, they are not as serious about dying. Although it is true that adolescent girls more frequently attempt suicide and survive, any previous attempt should be considered a prime risk factor for eventual completed suicide. The chilling fact is that an individual who has made one suicidal gesture or attempt is more likely than the general population to try again. Whether male or female, the adolescent who has attempted suicide has acquired a potentially lethal coping mechanism. If treatment and aftercare are not effective, suicide is even more likely.

A young person coming out of a depressive episode in which suicide has been a concern is less likely to attempt or complete suicide. A significant percentage of individuals who kill themselves do so after a hospitalization in which they appear to be recovering. Posthospitalization is typically considered a high-risk period in the recovery phase of a previously depressed and suicidal individual.

Suicide attempts and completions reflect a weakness or character flaw. The erroneous belief that suicide reflects a weakness or character flaw is the same type of damaging perception held for decades about individuals suffering from alcoholism and depression. Suicidal behavior is preceded by certain symptoms that suggest a medical and/or psychological process. These conditions, although complex, can be diagnosed and treated just as other syndromes and predictable patterns can be.

Talking openly about suicide will increase the chance that an adolescent will make a suicide attempt. The opposite of this notion is generally true. When suicide is discussed compassionately, sincerely, and therapeutically, the troubled individual is usually relieved to know that someone cares. The presuicidal adolescent is confused and ambivalent about life. Therefore, a sensitive inquiry into the youngster's feelings, combined with a firm opposition to suicide as an option, can effectively combat the suicide spiral. Discussing suicide openly and confidently in the educational setting tends to reduce the fear and irrational concerns that vulnerable adolescents seem to harbor. This is particularly true when a classmate has attempted or completed suicide.

When an adolescent appears suicidal, it is best to leave the problem to professionals. Although people without specific training in suicide assessment and intervention should definitely not attempt amateur diagnosis or treatment, they must not ignore signs of trouble. Adolescents tend to share their suicidal thoughts and feelings with friends, teachers, and family members. It is extremely important that nonprofessionals know how to recognize symptoms, respond constructively, and refer the suicidal youth for professional help.

The tendency to commit suicide is inherited. Suicide patterns may appear in families, but such patterns are likely the result of familial depressive tendencies—suicide and depression are, in fact, linked. Suicidal behavior as such is not inherited. Unfortunately, belief in hereditary transmission of suicide potential may lead to a less vigorous stance against suicide.

This book presents information on adolescent suicide in six chapters. Specifically, chapter 1 provides an overview of the problem, discussing the incidence of adolescent suicide and offering related statistics. Chapter 2 looks into the probable causes of adolescent suicide—stressors of adolescence, family influences, and adolescent depression. Chapter 3, on assessment of suicide risk, describes the signals and symptoms of suicidal behavior, methods for assessment of risk factors, and strategies for evaluating the suicidal adolescent. Chapter 4 discusses intervention—first theoretically, in terms of general strategies, and then specifically, as it occurs in the school setting. Chapter 5 provides the model of the school crisis team (SCT), an apparatus that, if implemented properly, enables schools to respond to a crisis situation as efficiently and effectively as possible. Finally, chapter 6 discusses the stressors experienced by special populations of adolescents, whose unique needs must be considered separately in order to intervene effectively.

The primary focus of the book is identification and intervention. Suicide prevention is to some extent an overlapping process that occurs when systematic assessment and intervention are successfully implemented. Although specific prevention efforts are certainly of value, in the fourth volume of the *Report of the Secretary's Task Force on Youth Suicide,* Eddy, Wolpert, and Rosenberg (1989) recommend rigorous evaluation of such programs as well as caution in implementing them. These observers suggest that until adequate information about the potential success of prevention programs is established, programmatic efforts must proceed slowly. Therefore, although specific programmatic suicide prevention efforts do exist, they will not be discussed in this book.

Case examples are used throughout the book to illustrate important points. These examples are derived from stories and vignettes provided by parents, friends, educators, and, in some cases, adolescents who have survived suicide crises. Collected over a period of 10 years, each example was given to me with the understanding that it might someday be published. Although most of these descriptions have been changed slightly to prevent identification of the adolescent or the family, their content remains true to the original experiences.

It is important to point out before proceeding to chapter 1 that not all suicidal youngsters fit a predictable mold. Tragically, there are times when an adolescent chooses death over life yet provides few or no clues as to the reasons for his or her choice. No amount of training or reading can substitute for a person's sensitivity and caring for each unique youngster. I recommend that the reader apply the information in this book in the context of a genuine concern for all human beings. As I tell my students, when all is said and done, it is your intuition that tells you whether someone wants to live or die—not a book.

CHAPTER 1

Defining the Problem

To the casual observer, Jimmy was a fairly typical teenager—reticent, especially around adults, and a moderate achiever in school. He had few close friends, all of them quiet and unassuming around the tougher kids at school. According to his homeroom teacher, Jimmy kept mostly to himself. These traits are typical for younger adolescents and aren't necessarily reason for special concern or attention. That's why Jimmy's death was initially thought to be an accident. One dark weekday morning, while delivering papers on his bike, Jimmy suddenly swerved into the path of an oncoming truck and was killed instantly. At first police thought that the unsafe conditions—the darkness and light drizzle that made the road slippery—caused Jimmy to lose control of his bike. That was until a note describing his feelings of hopelessness and rejection was found in his school locker. Part of his note read, "Why me, why always me? They make fun of everything I do, everything I am. It's such a cruel punishment."

Jeanine was an ebullient 16-year-old. Her grades were good, and she was popular enough to be elected to homecoming court. She was regarded by the faculty as a model student and a fine representative of her school. Then, gradually, she became apathetic. Parents and teachers thought the change was only a temporary emotional "phase" that many young women go through. Her death by drug overdose shocked everyone. How could this lovely, popular young lady with a promising future do such a terrible thing? She left no note to explain the confusion. However, subsequent investigations uncovered the apparent cause: Jeanine had been rejected by three of her friends who became jealous of her success and popularity. They apparently started a rumor that Jeanine was promiscuous and had contracted a venereal disease. Feeling overwhelmed and isolated, Jeanine took what she thought was the only way out.

Unfortunately, cases like these are not uncommon. The number of young people in the United States who take their own lives each year is extraordinary. As cited in Peck, Farberow, and Litman (1985), Herbert Pardres, former Director of the National Institute of Mental Health, asserts:

We are said to be in the midst of an epidemic of adolescent suicide. Every city and community, from the tidy row-house neighborhoods of the northeast corridor to the affluent new suburbs of the Sun Belt, has its horror story of the bright young student with the unlimited potential who brutalizes the sensitivities of his or her family and friends with the most wanton act of self-abuse. In an epidemic, the statistics become stupefying. . . . But behind these statistics are the young people—sons and daughters, brothers and sisters, students and friends—who were not able to find a way out of their pain or confusion or loneliness. It is up to us to help those who have yet to face similar crises. (p. 18)

INCREASING RATES OF ADOLESCENT SUICIDE AND CHANGING SOCIAL INSTITUTIONS

Historically, adolescent suicide has accounted for about half of the suicides across all age groups. Then, around the mid-1950s, adolescent suicide rates began increasing steadily. In 1980, for the first time, adolescent suicide rates exceeded the average rate for all other age groups (see Figure 1.1).

Since 1960, the overall rate of adolescent suicide has more than doubled, with the greatest increase being noted in individuals between 15 and 19 (see Table 1.1). Suicide is second only to accidents as the leading cause of death in this age group. Some epidemiologists and suicidologists believe the figures would be even higher if the circumstances surrounding accidental deaths (e.g., vehicular deaths) were examined more carefully (Hafen & Frandsen, 1986). Proponents of this theory suggest that some accidental deaths may in reality have occurred due to a subintentional wish to die.

Younger children are also victims of depression and suicide. Although suicide is relatively rare in children under 14, during the early 1980s there were notable increases in the suicide rates in that age range. The late 1980s revealed decreasing then once again increasing rates (see Figure 1.2).

Holinger and Offer (1989) have found that the number of children between 5 and 14 who attempt suicide each year may be as high as 100,000. A 1985 Centers for Disease Control report suggests that the true number of suicides among young children is likely underreported. And Cohen-Sandler, Berman, and King (1982) suggest that as many as 12,000 children between these ages are treated in hospitals annually for depression and suicidal behaviors.

Figure 1.1   Suicide Rates for All Ages and Adolescents (15–24) per 100,000 Population in the United States (1900–1985)

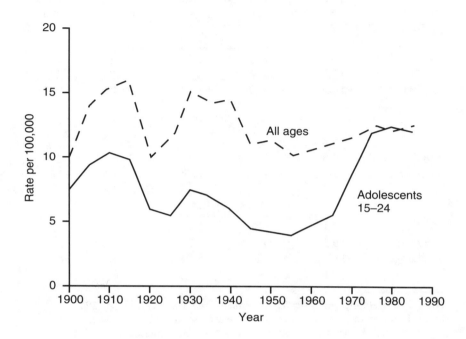

Note. From "The Emergence of Youth Suicide: An Epidemiologic Analysis and Public Health Perspective" by M. Rosenberg, J. Smith, L. Davidson, and J. Conn, 1987, *Annual Reviews of Public Health, 8,* p. 420.

Why are so many youths looking upon suicide as an option? Most writers do not propose a single theory but rather endorse the hypothesis that young people gradually become predisposed to suicidal thoughts and actions after a succession of traumatic events or debilitating conditions. Events and conditions most commonly associated with youth suicide are traumatic family life; chronic or acute stressors that represent important issues to a young person; major losses; and psychiatric conditions, including depression, personality disturbances, and substance abuse. These factors appear to interact and create emotional states that evoke feelings of hopelessness and despair.

Table 1.1 Suicide Death Rates for Years 1960 and 1987 (per 100,000 Population)

Year	All	White male	White female	Black male	Black female
		Ages	15–24		
1960	5.2	8.6	2.3	4.1	1.3
1987	12.9	22.7	4.6	12.9	2.5
% change	+148%	+163%	+100%	+214%	+92%
		Ages	15–19		
1960	3.6	5.9	1.6	2.9	1.1
1987	10.3	17.6	4.4	8.9	2.7
% change	+186%	+198%	+175%	+206%	+145%
		Ages	20–24		
1960	7.1	11.9	3.1	5.8	1.5
1987	15.3	27.5	4.7	17.2	2.4
% change	+115%	+131%	+51%	+196%	+60%

Note. From *Adolescent Suicide: Assessment and Intervention* (p. 19) by A. L. Berman and D. Jobes, 1991, Washington, DC: American Psychological Association. Copyright 1991 by the American Psychological Association. Reprinted by permission.

Adolescence has generally been viewed as a turbulent time for generations of people. Why the spiraling suicide rates now? It can be argued that current stressors are more complex and more numerous than they were for previous generations. But whether or not one agrees that the stressors are worse, it seems undeniable that today's youth feel that they have nowhere to turn for help with their troubles.

The phenomenon of lack of support for youth may be linked to larger social shifts. The past three or four decades have seen significant social and economic changes. As a result of these changes traditional social institutions—families, schools, friends, neighborhoods, and communities—have become more and more fragmented, transitory, and impersonal. It is a sad commentary on the state of our social institutions that, typically, suicidal adolescents perceive the world as uncaring, unresponsive, or hostile and wish to escape this intolerable, psychically painful situation.

**Figure 1.2   Rise in Suicide Rate Among Those Aged 5–14
in the United States During Selected Years (1960–1989)**

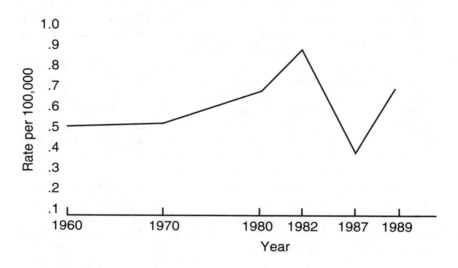

Note. Adapted from *Suicide in the United States: 1958–1982* (p. 150) by
the National Institute of Mental Health, 1985, Washington, DC: U. S.
Government Printing Office; and *Monthly Vital Statistics Report: Final
Data, 40*(8) (p. 21) by the National Center for Health Statistics, 1992,
Washington, DC: U. S. Government Printing Office.

SUICIDE ATTEMPTS AND THE REPORTING OF SUICIDES

Although the exponential increase in suicide completions for adolescents causes alarm, the increase in suicide *attempts* is mind-boggling. A
1991 Centers for Disease Control (CDC) study found that an estimated 3.6 million young people in the United States considered suicide
during the year 1990. That survey, the first time the federal government had collected data on attempted rather than completed suicides,
also found that approximately 2.1 million adolescents in grades nine
through twelve actually devised plans to take their own lives. Patros
and Shamoo (1989) estimate that approximately 1,000 teens attempt
suicide each day.

The data on number of attempts are conflicting, but the range is
from approximately 8% (Smith & Crawford, 1986) to 20% of selected

geographic samples of adolescents throughout the United States (Rubenstein, 1989). Lower estimates of 50 to 100 attempts for every completed suicide suggest that more than one-half million adolescents attempt suicide each year in this country. After lengthy hearings in 1985, the U. S. House of Representatives Select Committee on Aging concluded that suicide attempts by young people may have risen as much as 3,000% a year (U. S. Congress, 1985).

In the recent Gallup Survey on Teenage Suicide (Gallup, 1991) 45% of randomly selected adolescents aged 13 to 19 knew someone who had attempted suicide and failed. A total of 15% of those surveyed knew someone who had completed suicide. Similar findings resulted from a Midwestern survey of over 400 junior and senior high school students (see Table 1.2). This survey (Karolus, Kirk, & Shatz, 1990), like the Gallup survey, found that almost half of the students reported having a friend who had attempted suicide.

The rate of self-destruction among adolescents might be substantially higher when speculative data about unintentional or subintentional suicide are considered. The case of Jim, age 17, is typical: Jim was close to the top of his class academically and a lettered athlete in three sports. He expected scholarship offers from prestigious colleges. The family, school, and community were shocked when Jim's car plummeted off a bridge into the icy river where he fished often with his father and brothers. The coroner ruled Jim's death accidental, ignoring such signals as Jim's recent visits to the family physician about his fa-

Table 1.2 Suicide Attempts and Completions Known by Junior and Senior High School Students

	Suicide attempters	Suicide completers
Parent	3%	2%
Sibling	2%	1%
Other family member	11%	9%
Friend	47%	11%
Acquaintance	36%	24%

Note. From *Identification of Suicidal Symptoms by High School Students* (p. 2) by S. Karolus, W. G. Kirk, and M. Shatz, February 1990. Paper presented at the annual meeting of the Illinois School Psychologists Association, Champaign, IL. Copyright 1990 by the authors. Reprinted by permission.

tigue and weight loss, and his appointments with the school counselor to discuss being "down and out." The poetry found in his bedroom, referring to death as a "haven from the hassles of life," was never considered.

It is not easy to differentiate between a serious depressive episode and the typical discouragement often experienced during the teen years, yet a consultation with Jim's parents, counselor, and doctor would likely have revealed the seriousness of his psychological state. People simply didn't read the signs correctly.

Another problem associated with reporting a young person's death as a suicide is reluctance to stigmatize the family unless the evidence is totally incontrovertible. In Jim's case, the death was reported as accidental because of influence the parents had with the local coroner and medical establishment.

The Centers for Disease Control (1985) have underscored the possibility of judgment errors or prejudicial reports from certifying officials. Reasons for this, although not easy to document, likely involve one or more of three problem areas. First, criteria for determining a death a suicide vary from one state to another and cloud the national reporting census. Second, pressure to ease the pain of survivors may influence the judgment of the certifying official. This type of thinking must be understood in light of the fact that the certifying official is also a member of the victim's ecological unit. As such, there may be concern for the impact on school or community and the wish to avoid additionally burdening other survivors. Finally, suicide is determined as the cause of death more definitively and reliably when a suicide note is left. Adolescents who complete suicide infrequently leave notes, thus allowing room for conjecture (Peck, 1986). When events surrounding the suicide are ambiguous, it is easy to err on the side of compassion for the family and the memory of the young person. However, to deny the reality of a suicide also means to lose the opportunity for investigation that would help prevent other suicides.

SEX DIFFERENCES, METHODS, AND MEANS OF SUICIDE

Sex Differences

When suicide rates for the general population are considered, certain intriguing patterns emerge. Men generally complete the act of suicide at about four to five times the rate of women, but women attempt suicide about three to nine times as often as men. Reasons for this discrepancy between the sexes are not fully understood; however, choice of methods or men's fear of failing the attempt may partially explain it (Davis & Sandoval, 1991; Garfinkel, 1989; Ingersoll, 1989).

Methods

Males generally use more lethal methods than women and thus decrease their likelihood of survival (see Table 1.3). For example, adolescent males tend to use firearms more frequently than adolescent females, although young females appear to be showing an increased willingness to use more proactive methods, firearms included (Berman & Jobes, 1991; Boyd, 1983). The most common method by which females attempt suicide is the overdose, using drugs and poisons. The choice of drugs used in both attempts and completions tends to be either minor or major tranquilizers.

Means

Sloan, Rivara, Reay, Ferris, and Kellerman (1990) present interesting data demonstrating the relationship between availability of firearms and suicide attempts and completions. These researchers found higher suicide rates in geographical areas where legal access to firearms is easy.

Similarly, it can be conjectured that easy availability of drugs (either prescribed or nonprescribed) and poisons is also related to more

Table 1.3   Methods of Suicide: Ages 15–19 and 20–24 (1987)

Method	Ages 15–19		Ages 20–24	
	Total	Male:Female	Total	Male:Female
Substances	6%	1:7	6%	1:5
Gases	11%	1:1.3	10%	1:1.7
Hanging	19%	1.5:1	19%	1.8:1
Firearms	59%	1.4:1	59%	1.2:1
Other	4%	1:2.3	6%	1.05:1

Note. From *Monthly Vital Statistics Report*, *37*(13)(p. 12) by the National Center for Health Statistics, 1989, Washington, DC: U. S. Government Printing Office.

frequent suicide attempts and completions. As one school nurse remarked:

> Both times Beth overdosed, she was able to get her hands on pills so darn easily. It was her mother's meds the first time, and then she stole her boyfriend's father's lithium the second time. I know it sounds simplistic, but if she wouldn't have gotten her hands on such a powerful drug the second time I think she would still be alive.

TIME AND SEASONAL FACTORS

The time and seasonality of suicides has been studied in an attempt to determine possible temporal influences on a person's tendency toward self-destruction. Adult white males complete suicide more frequently in the spring, less frequently in the fall and winter months (Centers for Disease Control, 1985). Adult white females complete suicide more frequently during May and September. In general, adolescent suicides are distributed evenly throughout the year, although there is a slight peak in November.

Cluster suicides—suicides in which one suicide triggers off one or more suicides in a geographical area—occur more frequently in February (Davis & Sandoval, 1991). More adolescent suicides occur on Mondays, with self-destruction least frequently occurring on weekends (Hoberman & Garfinkel, 1988). College students attempt and complete suicides most frequently in October and February. (Notably, these months are close to the beginnings of school semesters.)

Like adults, adolescents may also be prone to suicide at the time of anniversaries or key dates, when those dates represent a previous trauma or unresolved loss. An increase in adolescent suicide attempts has been associated with such anniversary periods (Curran, 1987).

GEOGRAPHY AND LOCATION

There are significant geographical differences in the incidence of youth suicides. About a century ago, during the time of rapid industrialization, suicides—including adolescent suicides—occurred more frequently in crowded, urban centers. Presently, however, youth suicides appear to be more prevalent in the less populated states, as Table 1.4 shows.

The western states report the highest rates of adolescent suicide, with New Mexico, Alaska, and Nevada reporting almost twice the national average. Recent reports suggest that suicide rates are higher in

Table 1.4 Rates of Suicide (per 100,000) by State for 15–24 Year Age Group (1980)

8.6–12.1	12.2–15.7	15.8–19.3	19.4–22.9	23.0–26.5
Hawaii	Delaware	Florida	North Dakota	New Mexico
Nebraska	Texas	Colorado	Wyoming	Alaska
Maryland	Louisiana	Arizona		Nevada
Iowa	Washington	Montana		
New Jersey	California	Oregon		
Arkansas	Idaho	Vermont		
Illinois	Utah			
Indiana	South Dakota			
Kentucky	Minnesota			
Tennessee	Kansas			
North Carolina	Missouri			
Michigan	Oklahoma			
South Carolina	Ohio			
Georgia	Pennsylvania			
Alabama	West Virginia			
Mississippi	Virginia			
New York	Maine			
District of	Wisconsin			
Columbia				
Massachusetts				
Rhode Island				
Connecticut				
New Hampshire				

Note. From *Youth Suicide in the United States, 1970–1980* (p. 22) by the Centers for Disease Control, 1986, Atlanta: U. S. Department of Health and Human Services, Public Health Service.

those states among the general population as well (National Center for Health Statistics, 1992).

Wilkenson and Israel (1984) suggest that less populated areas may offer less interpersonal support than more urban areas. This lack of support may have been associated with the cluster suicides in Plano, Texas (Davidson & Gould, 1989), in which eight teens completed suicides within a span of 15 months. This small, undeveloped rural community of 17,000 was transformed, practically overnight, into a fast-paced suburban metropolis of over 100,000. The healthy, intimate contact that a small, congenial community would otherwise maintain was lost before the more formal institutions of a larger community developed. The isolation and lack of interpersonal engagement, however temporary, apparently affected the community in a dramatic manner.

Interpersonal isolation, whether it occurs on a Native American reservation in Wyoming or in a rapidly expanding suburb, can serve as a precursor to suicidal behavior. Conversely, the more populated states report fewer completed suicides, owing, it is suggested, to comparatively greater social integration.

CLUSTER SUICIDES

One of the more frightening and controversial phenomena in the last decade has been the clustering of suicides, also known as *suicide contagion*. Cluster suicides occur when more than one suicide completion or attempt occurs within a proximate geographical area and when these events appear related. The following two examples are typical.

Brett and Adam were typical high school buddies—they had become inseparable. Their parents didn't worry about them because they were involved in lots of constructive activities: yearbook, band, chess club, and the school newspaper. College-bound seniors, they had been accepted by the same prestigious university. Then suddenly, without any warning, they attempted a double suicide by asphyxiation. Brett died; Adam survived, brain damaged. The entire community was traumatized. Their tragedy followed the suicide of a young man in a neighboring community and two unrelated suicide attempts within a 30-mile area of town.

Robbie, a well-liked but generally unremarkable seventh grader, hanged himself in the park where he often played ball as his fellow playmates were engaged in the game he loved. There seemed to be no logic in his motivation, no previous symptoms that would have alerted anyone. He had, however, seen the film *An Officer and a Gentleman*, in which a naval cadet hangs himself in despair. Robbie's death was followed by the death 10 days later of Justin, a junior high school student. This student didn't know Robbie, but he also seemed vulnerable. He had been seeing the school psychologist, partly because of his parents' concern about his not "fitting in" with his peers. Justin hanged himself from a tree, like Robbie. In the ensuing weeks, four more young people killed themselves.

The links in cluster suicides seem to be geographical proximity, adolescent vulnerability, and the possibility of contagion. Such clusters are partially explained by the infectious disease concept. When a pathogen is introduced into a vulnerable population, the probability of infection is spontaneously increased. Similarly, when a suicide occurs and perhaps is reported sensationally, other young people who may already be in a state of helplessness or hopelessness may be influenced toward greater despair.

Controversy surrounding the contagion concept centers on the inability to demonstrate scientifically that one suicide attempt or completion directly influences another (Berman, 1989; Kessler, Downey, Milavsky, & Stipp, 1988). Indeed, critics go to great lengths to dispute any causal relationship between certain types of influences (i.e., television accounts of youth suicides) and actual suicides. Berman (1988), however, puts this phenomenon in perspective by stating that "there is little dispute that clusters do occur and that suicidal youths within a cluster have known risk factors that can identify them with some precision" (p. 105). The following excerpt from the mother of a suicide victim in the Midwest attests to this fact on a more personal level:

> I know for certain, for positively certain, that if the first
> suicide would not have occurred that my son would still be
> alive. Sure he had problems, but who doesn't at age 16?
> But it all seemed to happen around the time of that first
> death. He turned inward and we just couldn't seem to reach
> him. My God, what a waste!

Table 1.5 illustrates some clusters of adolescent suicides suspected to have been related to the contagion effect. The suicides in Wind River, Wyoming, are poignant examples of contagion. All of the deaths

Table 1.5   Recent Cluster Suicides in the United States

Place	Number of suicides	Ages	Dates
Plano, Texas	8	14–18	2/83–5/84
Westchester, New York, and Putnam County, New York	5	13–19	2/84–3/84
Clear Lake, Texas	6	14–19	8/84–10/84
Wind River, Wyoming	9	14–25	8/85–10/85
Omaha, Nebraska	3	15–18	2/3/86–2/7/86

Note. Adapted from "Contagion as a Risk Factor for Youth Suicide." In *Report of the Secretary's Task Force on Youth Suicide: Vol 2. Risk Factors for Youth Suicide* (p. 101) by L. Davidson and M. S. Gould, 1989, Washington, DC: U. S. Government Printing Office.

occurred by hanging within a 2-month period. The reasons offered for these calamities range from voodooism and cult activities to imitation, as in the case of Robbie. Peer behavior is a very forceful influence in the lives of adolescents—both positively and negatively. Thus, learning that a peer has given up the struggle can introduce the concept of self-destruction in a seductive and potent manner. As Shafii, Carrigan, Whittinghill, and Derrick (1985) conclude, "Exposure to suicide or suicidal behavior of relatives and friends appears to be a significant factor in influencing a vulnerable young person to commit suicide" (p. 94).

Other investigations into the contagion effect focus on the media. Phillips and Carstensen (1986) report a relationship between cluster suicides and how the news of a suicide is presented to the public. They found that the more sensational the reporting of the suicide (e.g., front-page headlines), the greater the increase in suicides within the reporting area. Surprisingly, they also found a significant increase in auto fatalities following the suicides, which provided some interesting momentum to the contagion theory. Another line of their research has followed the increase in adolescent suicides following certain made-for-television movies that focus on episodes in the lives of troubled and suicidal adolescents (Phillips & Carstensen, 1986). The films studied typically showed the suicide itself.

Although refuting this aspect of contagion theory, Berman (1988) cautions researchers and clinicians by suggesting that there are certain imitative effects with regard to methods of suicide. This, in part, is what was suspected in the Wind River deaths. I myself intervened with a 9-year-old boy who was discovered preparing to cut his wrists. When I later asked why he chose this particular method, he replied that he had seen it done on television.

Whatever the eventual outcome of the debate, it is clear that there is some sort of correlation, if not causation, in adolescent suicide. Until the facts are in, it may be best to proceed cautiously, as reflected in comments made by one associate newspaper editor:

> Whenever I hear of the suicide of a young person, I immediately call a consultation session with my staff. Knowing what I now know, I'm not about to heroize the act of copping out and maybe put the idea of self-destruction in some depressed youngster's head. We may treat it very clinically and factually, but no more splashy headlines.

SUMMARY

Adolescent suicide is a national epidemic that claims more lives each year. Individually, in "pacts" with friends, and in geographic clusters, an ever-increasing number of young people look upon ending their lives as the only solution to ending their pain. Changes in the larger society during the past 30 to 40 years—including the increasingly fragmented and impersonal nature of such social institutions as family, schools, and communities—have contributed to this national tragedy.

Variables influencing suicide completions and attempts (e.g., sex differences, methods and means, time and seasonal factors, and geography and location) have been identified. The phenomenon of cluster, or contagion, suicides, in which one suicide completion can trigger a spate of other suicide attempts and completions within a geographical area, must also be considered.

CHAPTER 2

Searching for Causes

In discussing a topic such as adolescent suicide, identifying causes is extremely difficult. Obviously, a host of contextual and individual factors determine whether or not an adolescent will actually attempt or complete a suicide. Despite the difficulty of determining exact causes, clues to identifying at-risk adolescents exist. This chapter identifies some of the main characteristics of adolescents' environments and personalities, and the relationships between the two, that may put them at risk for suicide.

The chapter is divided into three sections. The first section considers adolescent stress, ways of measuring adolescent stress, adaptation to stress, and what characteristics enable certain adolescents to succeed despite multiple and/or chronic stressors coupled with inadequate family and community support. Because of the family's importance in the life of the adolescent, the second section concerns the role of the family and family life. Finally, the third section focuses on depression as a precipitant of adolescent suicide.

ADOLESCENT STRESS

As David Elkind points out in his book *All Grown Up and No Place to Go* (1984), today's young people are encountering a multiplicity of unusual stressors that tax their ability to cope. Contemporary adolescents face stressors previously reserved for adults:

> From every corner of society our children are faced with forced blooming: if a child doesn't read by the age of four we label him or her a failure; television and the movies tell our young teens that sex is in and childhood is out; and parents increasingly look to a child to rescue them from the despair brought on by divorce, role conflict, and job dissatisfaction. These pressures and others are overwhelming our children. (p. 112)

According to Elkind, the consequences of these pressures can be disastrous. When adulthood is thrust upon young people without sufficient preparation, they face life with a porous identity, an underdeveloped defense system, and an increased susceptibility to physical, psychological, and spiritual damage.

Stress is a natural part of life. Adolescent suicide is not necessarily the result of stress as such, but suicide is directly related to vulnerabilities created by pressures with which young people are unable to cope. Our task is to help young people develop functional coping abilities and simultaneously to provide personal and social support as they experiment with those coping attempts.

Sources of Adolescent Stress

The origins of adolescent stress are varied because the constantly changing life of the adolescent is filled with losses. Although many adolescents look forward eagerly to the changes that mark adulthood, a concomitant loss of childhood stability and structure is manifest in changed relationships with parents and peers. A recent Gallup (1991) survey queried adolescents directly about the reasons they believed a teenager might think about committing suicide: Twenty-two percent answered that problems with growing up were responsible, 16% said peer pressure was responsible, and 14% said problems with parents were responsible.

The increased responsibility that comes with adolescence signals the loss of childhood freedom. The list of adjustments is quite long and represents the need to relinquish certain roles and activities in order to gain others. Table 2.1 presents some of the more common stressors adolescents face. This list has been adapted from Cohen-Sandler and Berman (1982); D'Arcy and Siddique (1984); Dornbusch, Mont-Reynaud, Ritter, Chen, and Steinberg (1991); Hendren (1990); and Walker and Green (1987).

Although almost any stressor could conceivably be linked to adolescent suicide, certain categories of stressors render the adolescent particularly vulnerable to extreme states of helplessness and discouragement. In addition to family influence, discussed later in this chapter, these categories concern physical change and development, peer relationships, and philosophical and spiritual conflicts.

Physical Change and Development

Although normal changes during puberty generally create stress for the adolescent, most young people adapt fairly well to this natural process. There is scant evidence that the process of puberty is a wholesale stress experience, although certain conditions can make it more stressful for some adolescents. A biological marker that seems to affect

Table 2.1 Stressors of Adolescence

Expected and normative

Pubertal growth
Physical changes and development
Intellectual and cognitive changes
Sexual growth and gender refinement
Changes in family relationships
Changes in peer relationships and peer pressures
Social expectations
Normative school changes (junior high, high school, college)
Academic pressures

Unexpected and extreme

Physical illnesses and/or accidents
Disfigurement or unusual physical challenges
Exceptional developmental delays
Multiple family relocations
Parental separation, divorce, or death
Death or serious illness of a friend or acquaintance
Sexual/physical abuse, neglect, or exploitation
Parental pathology (alcoholism, mental illness)
Arrest, probation, or jail term
Sexual problems or dysfunction

---

boys critically, for instance, is significantly late physical maturation. Vocal tone, facial hair, and the more obvious signs of manhood are important hallmarks in the adolescent male community, and not keeping up with one's peers developmentally may be stressful. Psychobiological research focusing on adolescent female markers has determined that stress during puberty in girls is related to excessive production of the steroid androstenedione (Nottleman, Susman, Inoff-Germain, Cutler, Loriaux, & Chrousos, 1987).

Peer Relationships

Interpersonal stressors occurring among peers can range from mildly debilitating to chronically devastating. The process of separating from parents, coupled with emerging dependence on peers, is both exciting and distressing to the majority of adolescents. Self-esteem, so precarious during this time, may be dependent upon whether one is accepted by a team or the right group.

Peer problems are highly influential in the development of suicidal ideation among young people (Dashef, 1984; Gore & Colten, 1991). Most youngsters make it through this period relatively unscarred in spite of rejection and exclusion, but suicidal youngsters perceive their peers to be inordinately important and thus become hypersensitive to nonacceptance (Topol & Reznikoff, 1982). Even young people who are accepted by their peers may be suicidal simply because they cannot or do not allow themselves to internalize their acceptance. They seem to live with a constant sense of incompetence and failure. Curran (1987) suggests that such teens are failures to themselves and are only superficially involved and invested in their peer group.

Philosophical and Spiritual Conflicts

Although not much is written about the role of values and personal philosophy in relationship to stress and the stress response, this factor may play a role in adolescent suicide. Parents with a deficient philosophical framework may provide poor models for their children, who in turn fail to develop a healthy framework from which to conceptualize the world and are consequently less able to cope.

According to Adams (1980), spirituality can be defined theologically or philosophically and implies basic questions essential in working with any age group. These questions, challenging for the mature adult much less for an adolescent, are "Who am I?" "Where am I going?" and "How am I going to get there?" Adolescents who have reasonable answers to these questions tend to experience less stress and strain during their transition to adulthood. The development of a philosophy of life—and death—serves as an internal guidance system. Such a philosophy is critical when one encounters challenges and pressures.

Young people need help developing guidelines and attitudes that will assist them in times of change and stress. Adams, in his holistic approach to stress management, maintains that this spiritual dimension can be the "glue" that facilitates the integration of our physical and psychological stress response. The influence of taking care of ourselves physically and psychologically has implications for the development of our spiritual/philosophical framework. Reciprocally, the nurturance of our spirituality directly influences whether we experience mental and physical well-being or illness and anxiety.

Adams's schema implies that common stress reduction strategies such as exercise, nutrition, rational thinking, and relaxation need to be integrated into a spiritual or philosophical framework. Whatever one's religious or philosophical orientation, it is important to realize that the answers to many of life's burdens and stresses lie not in a quick fix but in thoughtful personal integration.

Measuring Stress in Young People

One of the most common methods of defining those stressors most likely to cause breakdown has been the measurement of specific life events and correlation with illnesses that follow those events. Holmes and Rahe (1967) pioneered the Social Readjustment Rating Scale, proposing that when an individual endures a multitude of stressful experiences, the probability of developing physical problems increases. The scale includes positive as well as negative life events and is used extensively in stress and health research. The Stress Test for Youth presented in Table 2.2 includes items seen as stress producing for adolescents. The items perceived as most stressful appear first; subsequent items reflect a decreasing degree of stress.

Scoring of this stress test is relatively simple. A score below 150 generally reflects a normal stress load; a score of 150 to 300 or above would indicate a higher than normal level of stress, which might be predictive of eventual physical and mental symptoms. This version can be potentially helpful in determining a gross degree of stress but has not been validated, as has the Social Readjustment Rating Scale developed by Holmes and Rahe.

The Holmes and Rahe scale and others like it provide some indication of the relative weight of certain stressful events and conditions. This type of stress measurement also demonstrates how critical change is in the degree of stress: Experiences involving multiple changes in succession represent maximum stress. What is not measured in this type of scale is the duration of the stress event. The longer the stress exists, the more taxed the coping ability of the adolescent. The reader will also note how important the loss of social support is. The first five stressors listed in Table 2.2 represent a potentially lethal deprivation within the support system; this deprivation exacerbates the trauma of each stressor.

When an adolescent experiences a multitude of stressors culminating in major change, a common response is to feel helpless and defenseless. When major and repetitive pressures occur, the adaptive ability of the adolescent is severely compromised. Lee's case illustrates the effects of such multiple stressors upon a vulnerable youth: Lee was 12 when his parents filed for legal separation. He felt betrayed and abandoned. He remained with his father while his younger brother and older sister lived with his mother. During the summer, Lee's father left him with his paternal grandparents during working hours. Lee quickly developed a powerful attachment to both grandparents. Tragically, Lee's grandfather was diagnosed with incurable cancer and died by the end of the summer. Lee's parents continued a clumsy and conflict-ridden divorce negotiation, often bringing the children into their bickering. Lee's increasing isolation and withdrawal were not noticed

Table 2.2   Stress Test for Youth

Stressor	Points	Youth Score
Parent dies	100	_____
Parents divorce	73	_____
Parents separate	65	_____
Parent travels as part of job	63	_____
Close family member dies	63	_____
Personal injury or illness	53	_____
Parent remarries	50	_____
Parent fired from job	47	_____
Parents reconcile	45	_____
Mother goes to work	45	_____
Change in health of a family member	44	_____
Mother becomes pregnant	40	_____
School difficulties	39	_____
Birth of a sibling	39	_____
School readjustment (new teacher/class)	39	_____
Change in family's financial condition	39	_____
Injury or illness of a close friend	38	_____
Starts a new or changes an extracurricular activity (music lessons, Brownies, etc.)	36	_____
Change in number of fights with siblings	35	_____
Threatened by violence at school	31	_____
Theft of personal possessions	30	_____
Change in responsibilities at home	29	_____
Older brother or sister leaves home	29	_____
Trouble with grandparents	29	_____
Outstanding personal achievement	28	_____
Moves to another city	26	_____
Moves to another part of town	26	_____
Receives or loses a pet	25	_____
Change in personal habits	24	_____
Trouble with teacher	24	_____
Change in hours with baby sitter or caretaker	20	_____
Move to a new house	20	_____
Change to a new school	20	_____
Change in recreational or play habits	19	_____
Vacations with family	19	_____
Change in friends	18	_____
Attends summer camp	17	_____
Change in sleeping habits	16	_____
Change in number of family get-togethers	15	_____
Change in eating habits	15	_____
Change in amount of television viewing	13	_____
Birthday party	12	_____
Punished for not "telling truth"	11	_____
Total score		_____

Note. From "The Social Readjustment Rating Scale" by T. Holmes and R. Rahe, 1967, *Journal of Psychosomatic Research, 11,* p. 212. Copyright 1967 by Pergamon Press Ltd., Oxford, England. Adapted by permission.

because family members were experiencing the sadness and grief related to the death and the family rupture. It wasn't until Lee was discovered in the junior high school bathroom gouging his wrists with a cafeteria fork that teachers and family members realized how despondent he had become.

Adaptation to Stress

Adaptation (or *adjustment*, as it is sometimes called) refers to the process of meeting the critical requirements of a given situation at any given time. During final exams, for instance, the adaptive student puts a reasonable amount of time into preparation and study. Adaptation in this case means meeting the requisites of the external demand—namely, passing the exam. However, when an adolescent does not possess these adaptive abilities, unchallenged stress can lead to the exacerbation of physical disorders and psychological disturbances.

Physical Responses to Stress

Young people have been found to be at health risk when confronted by constant stressors. During adolescence the body is adjusting to the typical changes of puberty. This process alone can drain an adolescent of the physical and psychological reserves necessary for stability and growth. However, when chronic stressors and pressures (e.g., parental divorce, abuse, or even constant academic demands) occur, the body will eventually reach a point of fatigue and exhaustion. Hans Selye (1976), the father of modern stress research, formulated the stages that an individual will experience during the stress response and that can lead to biological breakdown. These include the following:

1. Alarm reaction: The autonomic nervous system responds to the emergency and activates the body's defense system (i.e., by releasing adrenalin, cortisol).

2. Resistance reaction: The body puts out a maximum effort to sustain itself in the face of an emergency—an optimal biological adaptation.

3. Exhaustion and collapse: The body depletes its stores of emergency reserves and becomes more vulnerable to infection, disease, and disintegration.

Each adolescent differs in terms of his or her unique stress response, but eventually, in the face of chronic and constant stress, physical deterioration occurs. This may manifest itself in one of several ways. If a congenital predisposition (e.g., allergenic asthma) exists, the youngster's condition may worsen during times of extreme pressure. Because chronic stress will, over time, tend to suppress immunological functioning, victims tend to become "host organisms" more prone to disease and infection. Potential consequences for young people include aggravation and exacerbation of existing physical conditions, such as diabetes (Jacobson & Leibovich, 1984), migraine headaches (Barlow, 1984), asthma (Fritz, 1983), and possible structural and tissue damage (Eaton, Peterson, & Davis, 1981; Henker, 1984). Such damage could even lead to premature coronary heart disease in young people (Matthews, 1981).

Symptoms of stress may be manifested even by preadolescents, as in the case of Mindy: When Mindy, an 11-year-old, was brought to the clinic, she seemed to be a bright and cheery youngster. Her physician referred her due to her "exotic and unusual" tendency to experience stress. An intelligence test yielded an approximate IQ of 165, but personality testing painted a picture of an ambitious, impatient, inflexible, and jealous child. Mindy's parents were successful lawyers who constantly impressed upon her their ethic—work hard, work constantly, and do your utmost to succeed. However, they were quite busy with their careers, and they found even less time to spend with her when her younger brother was born. The parents strictly screened nannies, who also were encouraged to promote the parents' philosophy and discipline. Mindy remained at the top of her private school class but began to complain of stomachaches. Her parents dismissed this until the school nurse strongly suggested a physical exam. After tests it was determined that she had a duodenal ulcer.

Psychological Responses to Stress

The majority of stress researchers promote a model that focuses on mind-body interaction (e.g., Girdano & Everly, 1979). How much stress any child or adolescent can tolerate depends upon a number of variables—genetic predisposition, temperament, learning or conditioning, environmental issues such as family and friends, and perhaps even luck. But two variables seem instrumental in determining how the young person will respond to stress: perception of the event or stressor and the social supports and resources available.

Perception of the event or stressor. The perception of a stressor is a key component in determining whether a young person will respond negatively. If a typically threatening event is not seen as disturbing, the adolescent will not react defensively. If an adolescent generally feels inadequate or insecure, the likelihood of stress is enhanced. A key component in teaching young people to manage stress is therefore helping them maintain rational perceptions of their often tumultuous world.

Social supports and resources. Perhaps the greatest buffer against stress is the ability to access the social support system during times of excessive strain. During adolescence, transitional issues related to changes in the support system develop. Parents previously provided essential support, but the young person turns more and more frequently to the peer system. The adolescent who can balance supportive relationships with family and friends will typically have critical support during even the most difficult of times.

Although relationships can be a critical buffer against stress, they have also been shown to be related to adolescent suicidal behavior when they become the source of stress. Eyeman (1987), for instance, lists the more common stressors of adolescent suicide attempters as follows:

- Breakup with boyfriend or girlfriend

- Trouble with a sibling

- Change in parent's finances

- Loss of a friend

- Trouble with a teacher

- Change of school

- Injury or illness

- Failing grades

- Increased arguments with friends

Conflicts within the support system not only increase stress but also eliminate or neutralize pivotal systems that would otherwise help the youngster to tolerate strain. Gore and Colten (1991) underline this point by suggesting that healthy relationships are crucial in alleviating excessive stress during adolescent years.

Psychological Hardiness

Kobasa (1979) coined the term *psychological hardiness* after studying people who seemed inoculated against stressors related to physical impairment. Her research led her to identify three personality attributes, which she termed the "3-Cs" of psychological hardiness: internal locus of control, commitment, and challenge. They and other traits of hardy adolescents are discussed here.

Internal Locus of Control

When an adolescent gives power and control to the environment and peers, he or she tends to experience increased stress, which results in an eventual compromise of physical and psychological integrity. Such relinquishment of personal control is often manifested in the message "Tell me who and what to be and I'll be it, even if it violates what I know is right." Because peer pressure is often the culprit in this trap, it is important to teach young people to be masters of their own fate. Most recently, this concept is being taught in drug and sexual abuse programs. At the heart of the matter is the ability to develop a sense of autonomy and yet achieve a meaningful and healthy reciprocity with others.

Commitment

A reasonable level of involvement in healthy, meaningful activities (music, chess, sports, drama, school newspaper, volunteer work, etc.) is also related to hardiness. Young people need to vary their activities and find diverse modes of expression. The opposite can lead to what Girdano and Everly (1979) call *deprivational stress*. Boredom, they contend, is related to depression and may affect as much as 20% of adolescents in the United States. They suggest that deprivational stress can easily lead to self-destructive behaviors, including drug abuse and suicide. The task, then, is to encourage and model healthy participation in life.

Challenge

Kobasa (1979) found that hardy and thus healthier individuals perceived many stressors as challenges. The perception of the stressor is therefore essential. Is not making the track team a reason to find a better use for your time or a reason to withdraw? Can joining the debating society offer an exciting opportunity or a reason to feel dread and anxiety? Kobasa suggests that the tendency to perceive stressors as challenges can be learned and polished—that it is not the result of temperament or heredity. The goal for parents, teachers, and mentors is to help young people view life as a series of stimulating challenges rather than obstacles.

Other Traits of Hardy Adolescents

Why do some children and adolescents thrive even in squalid and defeating environments? Again, researchers have investigated some of those youngsters who seem to grow in spite of psychotic or alcoholic parents, little or no support, and environmental constrictions that would challenge even the most healthy adult. Elkind (1981) lists the qualities identified by E. J. Anthony and Norman Garmezy as being linked to interpersonal growth: social competence, impression management, self-confidence, independence, and achievement. Essentially, these qualities describe young people who are at ease and perhaps thrive in most social situations. They possess an ability to master challenging situations as well as a need to "produce" and achieve. Many of their interests were crystallized as children, yet they remain eager to learn and are thirsty for knowledge. They tend to be interdependent—not overly dependent on the crowd but able to accommodate themselves and their social counterparts. They can appreciate adults while still relishing their own junior status and can appreciate privacy and peace, which apparently give time for contemplation and meditation.

THE FAMILY

The American family as an institution has been undergoing major structural and functional changes for many years. John Naisbitt, in his book *Megatrends* (1982), suggests that the traditional family arrangement so common 20 years ago—a father, a mother, and children with an extended group of grandparents, uncles, aunts, and cousins—is quickly vanishing. Today, he writes, the typical family might be "single parents . . . [or] a two career couple with no children, a female breadwinner with child and househusband, or a blended family that consists of a previously married couple and a combination of children from these two previous marriages" (p. 122).

Underlying these permutations, Elkind (1984) suggests, is the most striking change—the transition of the guardianship of children. The family is now sharing primary influence with, or surrendering to, other institutions in our society at increasingly early stages in the development of the child. Less and less information regarding living skills and social and personal values is being passed from parents, grandparents, or extended family members. Increasingly, children's social, academic, cultural, and religious/moral education is left to the media, peers, schools, and other social institutions. The lack of a central source of guidance and values increases the adolescent family member's psychological risk.

Certain family influences and stressors have been found to be related to adolescent problems in general and to suicide in particular (Cappuzi, 1986; Jacobs, 1971; Pfeffer, 1981). Often it is impossible to tell whether these influences were causes of the problems or symptoms of them. Did the family system create the adolescent's predisposition toward suicide, or did the family structure and atmosphere change in response to the adolescent's gradual decline? Regardless, family influences have been found to be related to adolescent suicide.

The Family as a System

The family can be thought of as a system in which family members exert a certain influence on the system and the system itself depends heavily on an internal balance. Parents are considered the chief architects of the family system and provide the structure, rules, and norms by which the family conducts typical business. This clearly defined way of conducting business provides direction and stability for the children, who are expected to abide by the rules and integrate family values and requisite behaviors into their lives. The values and norms of the family system usually approximate the values and norms of the larger society in which the family members participate, both as a group and as individuals. When these elements are in place, the family is considered balanced or functional.

However, the family system is not static. It is a changing, dynamic structure affected by both internal and external pressures. Therefore, a functional family can become unstable when beset by a crisis or problem to which it cannot adjust. If the family continues to be unable to adjust to the crisis, it becomes dysfunctional. On the other hand, a dysfunctional family can become functional if it begins working toward resolving the crisis or problem that made it dysfunctional. For example, an alcoholic parent who is the source of instability in a family might seek treatment. With the source of instability removed, the family might be able to address their other problems (e.g., the effect of alcoholism on the spouse and children) and work toward stability. In short, family stability/instability is fluid, operating on a continuum.

Influences within and pressures on both functional and dysfunctional families can undermine the development of the adolescent. These influences and pressures will be discussed specifically as they relate to adolescent suicidal behavior. Some might affect the adolescent directly and intensely (e.g., sexual and/or physical abuse), whereas others may be indirectly associated with the attempted or completed suicide (e.g., divorce or chaos in the family). Case studies and analyses will be presented to highlight major diagnostic themes and remedial strategies.

The Parent-Adolescent Relationship

Both parents and adolescents often retrospectively report that parent-child conflicts during adolescence were disruptive and memorable (Pearlin & Lieberman, 1979). These inherent conflicts are typically reciprocal and part of the normal process of growing up. Smetana, Yau, Restrepo, and Braeges (1991) found that both parents and adolescents tend to experience a relatively high degree of stress during this time, but that stress does not necessarily lead to unusual or pathological responses. However, unresolved parent-adolescent conflicts lend themselves to more dangerous problems.

Independence or Interdependence

A fair amount of research reports the adolescent years to be as, if not more, stressful for parents than for their offspring (Offer, 1969; Olson, McCubbin, Barnes, Larson, Muxen, & Wilson, 1983). A particularly sensitive area for both parent and adolescent concerns the issues of independence and separation. The developing adolescent appears to proceed, often awkwardly, through the phases of pseudoindependence, independence, and, finally, healthy interdependence.

The initial process of separating from parents is often handled poorly by both parent and child. The adolescent needs parental assistance and structure but overtly appears to resent and oppose this help. The adolescent also needs a certain amount of independence or separation from the parent. As mutual awareness of the necessity for separation develops, the adolescent will often exaggerate the move toward freedom and develop a life-style that only appears to be truly independent. This tendency is humorously embodied in the letter from a college freshman that in one sentence expresses independence and individuality and in the next sentence requests money.

If the maturing adolescent and the decreasingly threatened parent negotiate these inherent conflicts successfully, a gradual appreciation and acceptance of each other's roles develops. This phase is marked by true interdependence, characterized by an appreciation of mutual and acceptable dependency needs. One college student had this to say about the process:

> I was such a pain in my parents' lives. I just had to push forward, I guess, and I resented every attempt on their part to restrict or limit me. It was a miserable time for both of us. My therapist told me that I was really depressed—she called it "masked depression." We're now really enjoying a new relationship, and I can finally appreciate who they are and how important they are to me now.

Ideally, parents as tutors recognize the separation process for what it is—namely, a normal drive toward autonomy. That recognition can facilitate acceptance and support. When parents are threatened or unaccepting of the typical behaviors that emerge during this period, major conflicts often develop, communication channels break down, and the adolescent loses a critical component of the support system. The results can be potentially disastrous, as the following quote from the mother of a 16-year-old suicide attempter illustrates:

> Jamie always pushed for independence, and at times we
> felt like we did let go. When I look back on it, we really
> didn't. I think we both hovered over him and tried to pro-
> tect him. It backfired, and our relationship deteriorated. He
> ran away twice before he attempted suicide the first time.
> Of course, then we had even more difficulty in letting go.
> Therapy didn't really work until after the second attempt.
> It took 2 hard years, but we're on the right track now.

Admittedly, the parent-child relationship is one of the most critical in a young person's life. Even when parents are indirectly culpable by neglect or omission, it is antitherapeutic and counterproductive to place blame on survivors. It is not always true that the suicide completor had a dysfunctional family. In addition, because even adaptive and supportive families are often in states of flux, the distinction between functional and dysfunctional is not always easy to make.

The case of Tony involves stress originating in the family: Senior year in high school is typically an exciting time for young people— college or a career is on the horizon. But things were different for Tony. In his sophomore year, his father developed severe bouts of depression that required hospitalization approximately twice a year. Therapy, medication—even shock treatment—didn't seem to help. By the end of Tony's junior year, his father's insurance had run out, and the family finances had been exhausted. Tony had to take on two jobs. His summer vacation was a lost cause—he had planned a canoeing trip with friends but couldn't arrange for a replacement at either job. His plans for going away to college were scrapped in favor of attending the local community college part time. His mother now worked full time, and the younger children were farmed out to family and friends. Everything seemed out of kilter. Tony began resenting his father and noticing how his mother had become much more dominant and in control. He admired her more now, though, and she leaned on him for emotional as well as financial support. Tony even noticed how he began to play "father" to his two younger brothers. When senior year began in late August and Tony's friends began filling out applications for the state university, he began to feel discouraged and despondent. He became uninterested in socializing and was overwhelmed by a sense of futility. He was fatigued from lack of sleep and was losing weight. His girlfriend talked him into an appointment with the school counselor, who immediately referred him to his family doctor. Tony was found to be depressed and confused about his future and to have fleeting thoughts of suicide. Tony's mother was called, and the entire family was referred to a family counseling agency.

Tony's family became increasingly unbalanced by his father's health problems and the resulting role changes in the family. Out of necessity, Tony and his mother inherited the breadwinning roles. Certain psychological functions previously reserved for the marital partners were now shared by mother and son, and both began to experience personal change in response to their efforts to rebalance the family. All of this took its toll, particularly on Tony, whose developmental and personal needs were thwarted by the premature parental and financial responsibilities thrust upon him.

It is important to note that Tony's family was not directly responsible for his depression. Underlying the family stressors was, perhaps more central to the problem, Tony's own inability to communicate with anyone who could help him. Although he never said anything to anyone, fortunately his increasing frustration and feelings of hopelessness were detected early.

Communication Problems in the Family

Communication between parents and children is necessary for both parties to negotiate basic living and adjustment issues satisfactorily. Both verbal and nonverbal communication patterns promote good or ill health, nurturance (love and affection), or pathology (neglect and abuse). Certain family communication patterns have been thought to lead to confusion and eventual psychological disorganization (Bowen, 1960), and certain communication problems have been specifically related to adolescent suicide (Curran, 1987). Abraham (1978) states that suicidal adolescents may be the products of a suicidogenic family system where communication is very restricted, particularly with regard to openness and sensitivity to others. Specifically, families of suicidal adolescents are characterized by the following problems.

Communication barriers and ineffectiveness. The ability to negotiate both the trivial and monumental moments of life depends on the ability of the parent and child to talk openly and freely. Suicidal adolescents as a group tend to be deficient in their willingness and/or ability to communicate with their parents (McKenry, Tishler, & Kelley, 1982).

Two potential antecedents of suicidal behavior are reflected in communication barriers with parents. One concerns the adolescent who feels unable to communicate helplessness and hopelessness directly to parents. Jacobs (1971) found that the majority of adolescent suicide attempters in his study reported their attempt to friends first. The parents were then made aware of the attempt by the friend—not their child.

Negative and damaging statements. A second communication issue is reflected in the negative and damaging statements that some parents make to their teenagers. Messages that reflect excessive criticism and even dislike undermine the young person's already shaky self-concept. The following are examples of ineffective messages:

- You've got life so damn easy. Wait till you have to work for a living.

- Ask your teachers: They've got all the answers.

- Not in my house, you won't.

- I wish you'd be more like your friend, Alex. At least he's got his head on straight.

- What do you want now?

When parents communicate their disdain or dislike of a teen's behavior, it may be understood as a global insult or "put-down." When parents are the source of such a hurt, their offspring must look elsewhere for nurturance and support, but they have been made less competent to do so by the unhealthy modeling provided by their parents.

It need not necessarily be the content of the message that confuses or angers the adolescent: It can be the manner in which the message is delivered. The tone of voice of an impatient teacher, an angry parent, or an uninterested coach may be all that is needed to put off a sincere attempt by the youngster to make contact.

Arguments and rejection. An analysis of interactions between suicidal teenagers and their parents suggests that significantly more arguments take place in this group than among nonsuicidal adolescents and their parents (Hawton, 1982). Suicidal adolescents also perceive their parents to be much more rejecting than do disturbed but nonsuicidal teens (Topol & Reznikoff, 1982). When families are beset by turmoil and do not have the communication skills to resolve conflicts in healthy ways, a volatile and painful family atmosphere may be the result.

The following are examples of argumentative and rejecting messages:

- Way to go, hotshot. Let's see if you can screw up another one.

- You're just like your father. You'll never amount to anything.

- We're betting that you can't do it anyway.

- Absolutely not. Because I said no!

An accumulation of these kinds of negative messages becomes an increasing psychological burden that may be too painful for a young person to live with.

Inappropriate discipline and unhealthy modeling. Suicidal adolescents are sometimes the objects of intense discipline (Jacobs, 1971), including such ineffective and damaging strategies as yelling, nagging, criticizing, and physical punishment. Often the disciplinary measure does not fit the infraction. This type of parenting can create despondency and a feeling of helplessness in young people. The parents—the primary support system—become the adolescent's adversaries. This situation produces a painful environment the adolescent wishes to escape or avoid. As one 15-year-old boy commented, "Every time I turned around, my parents were on my back. Once I was grounded for a month just for coming in late. I had to run away—I didn't feel like I had any option."

Some suicidal adolescents also perceive their parents as "very unhappy, arguing individuals, who could hardly be models of loving, hopeful, coping adults" (Smith & Crawford, 1986, p. 317).

In summary, adolescents need stability in their lives and healthy models to emulate as they struggle with the difficulties of growing up. Ineffective communication, critical parental attitudes, inappropriate discipline, and unhealthy adult modeling may serve as possible antecedents to suicidal behaviors.

Mental Health Problems in the Family

Major mental health problems in the family also create a high-risk environment for the adolescent family member. Families with substance abuse, psychiatric disturbance, and physical or sexual abuse patterns have all evidenced a higher incidence of adolescent suicide attempts and completions (Jacobs, 1971; Shafii et al., 1985).

Substance Abuse

A critical component of healthy childrearing is the ability to model adaptive living patterns. The opposite, of course, occurs when parents consistently model maladaptive patterns such as alcohol or drug abuse. The exposure to substance abuse seems to create a vulnerability related to suicidal behavior. The families of adolescent suicide victims are often also victims of the substance abuse patterns of another family member (McKenry, Tishler, & Kelley, 1983).

The adolescent child of a substance abuser typically learns maladaptive coping strategies while simultaneously failing to learn modes of productive living. Much recent work concentrates on the children of alcoholics and the tremendous burden many of them shoulder (Doweiko, 1990; Johnson & Maile, 1987).

In addition, when an adolescent is raised in such an environment, he or she is more likely to develop substance abuse problems. Concomitantly, the risk of suicide increases, as the following case illustrates: Mickey's father wasn't a stereotypical falling-down drunk, but Mickey, age 16, knew his father had a drinking problem. Mickey's father drank from the time he got home from work until bedtime and began drinking before noon on weekends. But he wasn't openly abusive, he brought home the paycheck, and he went to church. Mickey began to ignore him, as adolescents often do with parents. Mickey's parents didn't seem to notice when Mickey came home tipsy after weekend parties, nor did they notice when he began sneaking alcohol from the family liquor supply. After all, there were cases of beer and liquor stored downstairs. They did notice when the school called about Mickey's absenteeism, but after a stern lecture, Mickey was right back at it. As he gradually slipped into episodes of discouragement and depression, Mickey continued to numb his feelings with more alcohol and then marijuana. When his friends confronted him, he changed crowds; when his ex-girlfriend tried to intervene, he hit her. He didn't mean it, he explained, he just didn't have control over his temper anymore. It was after that encounter that he finished a fifth of whiskey in the basement of his home, took his father's truck, and drove into a train at a nearby railroad crossing. Two witnesses saw him wait at the crossing until the train approached and then pull out into its path.

Although Mickey's death may have been more impulsive than many adolescent suicides, the earmarks of depression and the use of drugs to self-medicate depression are common. In this case, Mickey's father modeled a pattern of alcohol abuse that, because it was not publicly disruptive, allowed the family to appear functional. Nobody in the family confronted his father, and the alcoholic pattern was never openly discussed. Mickey's family represents a closed system—one that became relatively impermeable to healthy outside input.

When parents shut the family off from the outside world, the motivation to do so is often based on the need to protect a sick or deteriorating family system. In this case, the father's addiction and the mother's codependency caused them to adopt a relatively classic pattern of dysfunction. Over time, Mickey's mother developed an adaptation to her husband's illness that included chronic helplessness and hopelessness, and in this way she helped perpetuate the father's addiction. Without treatment, Mickey's father's disease progressed. Mickey became victimized by the chronic modeling of maladaptive coping and was unable to develop healthy, adaptive adjustment behaviors. This double liability overwhelmed him during a critical time in his development. His only chance was the world outside the nuclear family. If extended family or friends had insisted on his receiving help or had consulted teachers, counselors, or professionals, Mickey might have been reached in time.

Psychiatric Disturbance

Ongoing controversy over the inheritability of psychiatric disturbances exists. However, whether one wishes to hold genetics or poor modeling in the family environment responsible, it is undeniable that the psychiatric disturbance of a family member has profound effects on others in the family.

When parents experience severe mental health problems such as schizophrenia or bipolar (manic-depressive) disorder, their offspring are at greater risk for experiencing those and other psychological disorders (Paykel, 1982; Shafii et al., 1985). This finding is noteworthy because when children are raised in such an environment, they generally lack the basic coping skills to negotiate life's typical stressors. This is perhaps the main reason that children of parents who have severe depressive and suicidal tendencies are themselves at high risk for depression (Pfeffer, Conte, Plutchik, & Jerrett, 1980).

Adolescent suicide attempters have a higher incidence of suicides within the family than nonattempters (Berman & Carroll, 1984; McKenry et al., 1982; Shafii et al., 1985). When a psychiatrically disturbed family member commits suicide, adolescent offspring are at even greater risk for suicide themselves (Kerfoot, 1979; Shafii et al., 1985). In this context, suicide may be seen as a way of escaping the complicated pain and grief resulting from the loss. In addition, in such an instance, suicide has been introduced into the repertoire of family coping mechanisms and thus becomes an option, as is reflected in the following comments of a 22-year-old-college senior:

> I remember how they tried to shield me from my mom's craziness. If only I would have been told more and maybe consoled more. I felt such a void, an emptiness I can't explain. My therapist told me later I spent a good part of my teen years being depressed. When Mom killed herself, I just wasn't prepared. No one could be, I guess. All I know is I woke up in the hospital after taking pills and drinking beer after beer after beer. I guess I wanted to die. I still don't know.

Physical or Sexual Abuse

Another family environment that represents a major assault on the well-being of a child or adolescent is one in which the child is physically and/or sexually abused. Given the simplistic yet realistic theory that a common motivation to take one's life is the desire to escape from an intolerable situation, it is easy to understand why an abused young person would see suicide as a way out. The shame and guilt felt by victims of such abuse further enhance their isolation, fear, and loneliness (Deykin, Alpert, & McNamara, 1985).

Abusive families model a host of unhealthy behaviors and attitudes: general hostility, unhappiness, community isolation, financial insecurity, and conflict proneness (Aldridge & Dallos, 1986; Garbarino, Sebes, & Schellenbach, 1984; Richman, 1984). When the abuse occurs during the child's younger years, negative emotions may be repressed. These repressed emotions may then resurface during puberty, often resulting in overwhelming confusion, guilt, and disgust.

The case of Adeline is representative of the repression of emotions that eventually come back to haunt the abuse victim: When she enrolled in college, Adeline, 17, thought her fears and nightmares would cease. It had been 4 years since her stepfather had been arrested for a variety of felony charges, all related to embezzlement. Both she and her mother were relieved. Her mother had apologized often enough about making a bad marriage choice, and Adeline never said anything about the abuse that went on for 3 years—abuse that devastated her.

At college, when Adeline tried to study she felt constant anxiety and tension. Any attempt by the other girls in her dorm to solicit social contact was met with feeble excuses. Her attractiveness and shy personality appealed to many boys, but she panicked about going out with any of them.

By the second semester Adeline felt as though her world was collapsing. She couldn't concentrate on her studies, and she began to miss classes. Her avoidance of the other girls was so obvious that they just gave up on her. Her dorm counselor referred her to the counseling center, where her therapist felt she had much deeper problems than she was willing to discuss. Her counselor, sensing unresolved problems with her mother, suggested a weekend at home.

Although she did go home, Adeline was unable to disclose anything about the past to her mother. This added to her feelings of futility and self-recrimination. After hours of rumination, she found herself staring at her own contorted face in the bathroom mirror, behind which she discovered a bottle of her mother's pain medicine. She was rushed to the hospital after her sister heard faint murmurs outside her door.

True classic cases are few and far between, but Adeline fits a pattern typical of abuse victims, whether that abuse is physical or sexual. Her tendency toward self-deprecation and low self-esteem was a hallmark of her gradual deterioration. Adeline's anxiety kept increasing, and her ability to maintain her facade gradually diminished. At the core was her frozen self—frozen by the shame of what she perceived as sexual collaboration, in spite of her helplessness, and frozen by her inability to disclose her plight. Her friends, family, and teachers were all concerned, but even when they showed that they sensed her desperation, she remained defended and blocked. Adeline's impulse to die peaked after she was unable to open up to her mother—the one person whom she trusted but simultaneously blamed for having been unable to protect her from such horrific experiences.

Further clinical analysis suggests that Adeline's symptoms were indicative of major distress and an emerging crisis state. The gradual behavioral and academic changes did not alert anyone because they developed over a long period of time and were all too easily assigned to adolescence and general family problems. Everyone thought Adeline would sort things out because she seemed basically a resourceful and talented girl.

Even gradual changes over time in a young person should be taken seriously. If any questions exist, a thoughtful and systematic inquiry should take place regarding the reasons for those changes. In Adeline's case, her stepfather's arrest, combined with her symptoms, should have been a red flag. Eventually, her mother admitted that she had sensed something was wrong but had denied her own fears that her husband could sexually abuse her daughter. The idea was too painful to entertain.

Major Losses

Sooner or later, loss is an inevitable part of life. Human beings have two basic tasks related to major loss: engaging in healthy grief work and finding some type of replacement for what has been lost. After experiencing pain and discomfort following a loss, an adaptive adolescent will eventually seek a substitute. But sometimes when an adolescent sustains an overwhelming loss (e.g., traumatic relationship break, death of a parent) or a series of minor losses (e.g., school suspension, rejection or humiliation, exclusion from a desired peer group), he or she feels an intense threat to his or her very existence. The literature abounds with descriptions of young people killing themselves in response to the loss of a friend, a parent, or even self-esteem.

Three major losses within the family organization are, under certain conditions, related to adolescent suicidal behavior: divorce and separation, death of a parent, and family relocation.

Divorce and Separation

Divorce and separation are commonplace in the United States, and there is little indication that the divorce rate is slowing. Current estimates suggest that a child under age 16 has a 50% chance of being from a family that has experienced divorce (Bumpass, 1984). Although divorce is generally described as a painful experience by the adolescents who suffer due to it (Wallerstein & Kelly, 1980), the psychological consequences of divorce on children and adolescents depend more on the emotional climate of the family prior to, during, and after the divorce than on the divorce itself (Ingersoll, 1989). In some cases, an adolescent may thrive after an abusive or dysfunctional parent leaves the home.

Divorce taxes the ability of all family members to cope with a new and perhaps traumatic situation. In some cases, when the divorce occurs at a critical developmental time or is marked by constant conflict, the damaging effects impair the stability and adjustment of the adolescent. In his review of causal factors in suicide and family issues, Curran (1987) suggests that the risk may be greater when adolescents have a negative perception of their parents' divorce and when marital dissolution is experienced in the context of other family problems. Because divorce is usually an attempt to resolve the conflicts of the marital partners, it is not surprising that family life is very unpleasant, if not chaotic, prior to the break-up.

Bart's case highlights how important it is for divorcing or divorced parents to reassure and remain attentive to their children: From the time he was 6 years old, Bart and his father had been inseparable. There was seldom a time when Bart's father was at home that Bart was not at his father's side helping him with chores or begging to play ball. His father was very accessible in those days, but everything changed when Bart's parents separated just after his thirteenth birthday. Bart thought that he had done something to cause the break-up, and no amount of reassurance from his mother would dissuade him. It didn't help when his father began to pull away, offering excuses when it came time to see Bart play ball or help him with his paper route or homework.

The change was subtle, but by the time Bart was 15, he could tell that things were just not the same. He felt rejection and pain. His grades slipped. He quit the baseball team and his paper route in a veiled effort to solicit attention from his father. His mother was so broken up by the divorce that her efforts to help her son were largely ineffective. Bart waited for his father to leave on a business trip before he broke into his apartment and killed himself with his father's shotgun. Bart's note communicated his anger and despondency: "Why did you ruin everything for me and Mom? I hate it this way. I hate you."

Parents are often caught up in their own pain and anger when a marital dissolution occurs. Bart's feelings of responsibility for the divorce and abandonment by his father seemed justified when his father began avoiding him. If the parents had sought professional help for themselves and their child, Bart's feelings of abandonment and despair might have been identified and dealt with.

All children of divorce can be considered at some psychological risk. They are vulnerable to feelings of hopelessness and abandonment.

Time, care, nurturance, and close monitoring are essential as they attempt to heal and understand the meaning of the divorce.

Death of a Parent

When divorce occurs, the adolescent has the potential to restructure new relationships with both parents. When a parent dies, the loss is permanent and often overwhelming. Coping mechanisms are typically stretched to the limit, given the adolescent's needs for nurturance and security. A young person's ability to cope with the death of a parent is dependent upon the mental health of the family system, as well as on the availability of an intact, long-term support system.

In the following case, the combination of a negative prior family history, parental death, and the mode of death combined to increase one adolescent's vulnerability to suicide: Cindy, 16, was esteemed by the faculty of her high school but thought to be too haughty and distant by most of her classmates. She didn't particularly mind that she was not a cheerleader or prom queen. She worked hard, had two close friends, and was an aspiring veterinarian. However, her mother wanted a socially prominent role for Cindy at school and viewed her chosen vocation with disdain. Cindy began to have periods of brooding and moodiness.

It was at that time that the conflicts with her mother began to escalate. She couldn't seem to do anything to please her mother, who resented the close relationship that Cindy enjoyed with her father. Arguments increased and had a consistent underlying theme that confused and angered Cindy: Her mother wanted her to do and be all the things that she herself had not done and been as a teenager.

Then, suddenly, Cindy's mother was diagnosed as having an advanced malignancy. She received intensive treatment, but the doctors did not hold out much hope. They recommended psychiatric consultation for Cindy's mother, who often had periods of despondency interspersed with angry, hysterical outbursts directed at those around her. Cindy's father felt that Cindy was affected the most by her mother's outbursts, but he was unable to protect her.

Within days after her mother's funeral, Cindy was hospitalized with what the psychiatrist labeled severe reactive depression. The focus of treatment was grief work, but it was decided to leave the relationship issues between Cindy and her mother for longer term, outpatient care. Cindy never made it to the first session after her release. She asphyxiated herself in the garage in her mother's car. Her note lacked clarity and organization but referred to both her anger toward and love for her mother.

In this case, the suicide occurred following a major loss, which served as the precipitating event. Unclear boundaries between Cindy and her mother contributed to the outcome. Cindy, like all adolescents, needed to define her identity within the family—to know who she was. Cindy's mother confused Cindy with messages about who and what she should be. This conduct amounted to psychological blackmail—a kind of "damned if you do and damned if you don't." To make herself happy, Cindy had to reject her mother's wishes and dreams. Unable to do that, Cindy tried to make her mother happy by sacrificing her own wishes, dreams, and sense of self.

A *psychological autopsy* was conducted for Cindy. This proceeding, usually convened by a coroner, is designed to gather information related to the psychological status or state of mind of the deceased. The information gained—often by interviews with family, friends, fellow students, or even witnesses—may provide critical clues in determining whether the death was actually a suicide and in establishing the motivation for the death. During the psychological autopsy for Cindy, a psychologist serving as an expert witness suggested that Cindy may have wanted to join her mother in death—a symptom of cognitive irrationality specifically precipitated by her mother's personality dysfunction. Fostering healthy patterns in adolescents demands healthy parenting: In this case, Cindy's father was either too weak, too overwhelmed, or too unskilled to buffer Cindy from her mother's deficient parenting pattern.

Family Relocation

Family relocation is stressful for everyone but particularly for adolescents, who are typically unsure of themselves and prefer the security of a familiar context. Often their feelings of loss at being displaced are as severe as those they experience during a divorce or the death of someone close to them.

The case of Marvin and Tommy underlines this point: Marvin was the middle child in a military family and seemed to be making his way smoothly through school on the military base. The fact that his father had been transferred three times didn't seem to have tarnished Marvin's resilience or his ability to make friends. In fact, the problem was the reverse: He and his newest friend, Tommy, were so close that both their families worried.

When Marvin's father accepted a transfer to a foreign country, Marvin protested so vociferously that his mother took him to a base psychiatrist. Given Marvin's history, the therapist thought that once the move occurred, Marvin would adapt as he had in the past. The therapist suggested some preventive sessions with a family social worker prior to the actual move. But as the time for the move approached, Marvin became increasingly obstructive, moody, and inaccessible. He and Tommy ran away, but police found them hitchhiking the next day.

Both families consulted the social worker, who made plans to work with each boy and have group sessions with each family. The day of the first scheduled session, the boys disappeared during the lunch hour. Later that afternoon, they were found in one of the families' garages. Tommy was dead from a self-inflicted gunshot to the head. Marvin was critically wounded in the chest but survived. The suicide note, written by both boys, described the move as unfair, proclaiming "that best friends should never be apart."

It was not easy to identify what distinguished these youngsters from other teenagers who protest a family move but eventually adjust. The investigation into Marvin and Tommy's suicide pact uncovered nothing substantially different about their relationship or life-style—no drugs, no family pathology, no major differences between them and other students. One of the boy's teachers suggested that this tragedy was simply a statement about family mobility and the inability of kids to cope with constant changes.

As the case of Tony and Marvin illustrates, families who create an atmosphere of risk for their adolescents do not have to have major pre-existing social or clinical problems (e.g., sexual abuse, psychological disturbance). Certain family patterns even among otherwise functional families may set the scene for adolescent stress and, thus, serious crisis.

ADOLESCENT DEPRESSION

Depression is, perhaps, the most worthwhile topic to explore when attempting to explain suicide. Depression overwhelms a person with feelings of hopelessness, despair, helplessness, and self-deprecation that, in combination, consume the sufferer's life force until the fatigue and psychic pain are so great that the only solution may appear to be death.

In general, research has validated the relationship between aversive life events, such as relationship traumas, and the onset of depression. Paykel (1982) systematically reviewed the literature investigating traumatic life events occurring prior to depression and concluded that those events frequently serve as precipitating factors. The very nature of a severe depressive state seems to propel a person toward self-destruction, and for a variety of reasons, adolescents seem vulnerable to an assortment of depressive disorders.

Vivid descriptions of depression have been recorded as long ago as the early Egyptians, Greeks, and Chinese. It is only recently, however, that the subject of depression as a clinical mood state among young people has been more thoroughly debated (Barrett, 1985; Hawton, 1986; Leder, 1987; Pfeffer, 1986). The following section will discuss depression typology, depression among adolescents as a clinical state, and genetic factors. Specific prevention and intervention strategies for depressed adolescents will also be described.

Types and Subtypes of Depression and Related Suicide Risk

The Diagnostic and Statistical Manual of Mental Disorders (DSM-III-R; American Psychiatric Association, 1987) now accepts the diagnosis of depression in children and adolescents. It applies the same clinical criteria established for adults in defining the subtypes of depression. The distinctions drawn between these subtypes are often helpful in determining the cause and course of treatment.

Adjustment Disorder With Depressed Mood

Included in the adjustment disorder with depressed mood category are the normal "blues" that many people experience. This state is precipitated by an identifiable stressor, such as a relationship trauma or other loss event. Common symptoms include depression, tearfulness, hopelessness, and a response to the stressor that seems extreme. Although the disorder is characterized by disruption and impairment in the individual's work or social life, this level of depression is rarely associated with suicidal thinking.

Mood Disorders

The distinguishing characteristics of mood disorders are "a disturbance of mood, accompanied by a full or partial Manic or Depressive Syndrome. . . . Mood refers to a prolonged emotion that colors the whole psychic life; it generally involves either depression or elation" (American Psychiatric Association, 1987, p. 213). Within mood disorders, some particular subtypes are helpful to know in order to provide diagnosis and determine the course of treatment.

Depressive disorders. *Dysthymia* (or depressive neurosis), has more severe depressive symptoms than adjustment disorder with depressed mood. In addition, the origin or cause of the depression may be unclear. A dysthymic disorder may last longer than an adjustment disorder and is, in fact, marked by the duration of the depression rather than its severity. Impairment in work, school, or social functioning can be mild but is noticeable.

As with dysthymia, the stressor or cause of a *major depression* may be unclear. Major depression is a serious depressive state characterized by its episodic nature and the extreme sadness, dejection, and even immobility experienced during the depressive episode. There is usually a return to premorbid levels of functioning between episodes. Although it is possible for an individual to have just one episode, it is more commonly a chronic condition, with episodes increasing in frequency as the individual gets older. The episodes may last for weeks or even months and usually require medical intervention such as antidepressant medication or even, in some cases, electroshock treatment. Intensive support therapy is also required.

Bipolar disorders. The stressors causing *cyclothymia* may be obscure, but the individual will have manifested the symptoms for at least 2 years. Chronic mood disturbances are a distinguishing characteristic of this disorder. The individual may be manic, manifesting readily recognizable mood shifts, although depression is not as extreme as during an episode of major depression. Substance abuse is common as the individual attempts to self-medicate. Although the mania may produce stages of high productivity in terms of work, these are counterbalanced by low-productivity "down" stages, and the individual will experience interpersonal and social difficulties.

The *bipolar disorder* combines the manic qualities of cyclothymia with the chronic and severe depressive episodes characteristic of major depression. Bipolar disorder is marked by drastic mood swings. It is an obvious condition because the behaviors that accompany the disorder are so extreme and irrational. The mood states may last for a long time and repeat. Even the most conservative writers allow that the disorder may be biochemical in origin. Treatment usually requires biologic intervention, such as lithium, and, in some extreme cases, electroshock treatment has been deemed appropriate.

Symptoms of a Depressive Disorder

It is important to recall that the types and subtypes of depressive states and disorders are on a continuum. All of the states involve some of the same symptoms with different degrees of severity or overlap. The following specific symptoms are characteristic of most of these depressive states:

- A loss of interest in activities and events that usually evoke a pleasurable response: The individual may be apathetic to what once gave him or her joy.

- Disrupted sleeping patterns: The individual may have trouble getting to sleep at night or may wake up very early and dwell obsessively on unpleasant and negative feelings.

- Changes in eating habits and appetite: The individual often has little interest in food or eating, and, if the condition persists, may begin to lose weight.

- Loss of energy, inertia, and listlessness: The individual has a general sense of physical and emotional apathy.

- Psychomotor agitation, such as constant fidgeting and physical restlessness: In addition to moving frequently, shifting, and appearing generally anxious, the individual seems unable to attend to any one activity.

- Concentration problems that lead to intellectual or thought disruption: The individual cannot attend to an intellectual task and may appear distracted or "spacey."

- Thoughts and/or comments related to dejection and unusually poor and negative self-evaluation: The depressed person will often make comments about how worthless he or she feels and repeat themes of self-devaluation and self-blame.

- Associated thoughts about suicide and self-destruction: The depressed individual may find these thoughts difficult to verbalize and express them through statements demonstrating a lack of self-worth, as just described (e.g., "I really don't deserve to have friends/parents/teachers").

- Separation anxiety, manifested in an exaggerated fear of leaving home or being abandoned: Generally seen in pre-pubescent children, this symptom often involves clinginess to parents, school avoidance or phobia, or obsessions related to the possibility that the parents may die or abandon.

Adolescent Depression and Adolescent Suicide

Depression is considered a risk factor in adolescent suicide behavior (Petersen, Compas, Brooks-Gunn, Stemmler, Ey, & Grant, 1993). Carlson and Cantwell (1982) reported that as many as 83% of young people experiencing suicidal thinking also display symptoms of depression. In a study of suicide attempters, Withers and Kaplan (1987) found three-quarters of adolescents in their sample to be significantly depressed. Kovacs and Puig-Antich (1989) report an extremely high rate of suicide among adolescents experiencing major psychiatric disorders, including bipolar disorder, major depression, and schizophrenia. The majority of the completed suicides studied carried a diagnosis of either bipolar disorder or major depression. Not all adolescents experiencing depression, however, are necessarily suicidal (McWhirter &

Kigin, 1988). Although a depressive profile (i.e., feelings of hopelessness and despair) in and of itself is commonly related to suicidal thinking, it does not automatically lead to suicidal behavior. Other stressors, such as conduct disorders, severe family disturbances and dysfunctions (Kosky, Silburn, & Zubrick, 1986), substance abuse (Schuckit & Schuckit, 1989), and sexual abuse (Shafii et al., 1985) have been found to be related to both depression and suicidal behavior in young people. The discussion here will focus on depression as a condition predisposing the adolescent to suicide and will also detail strategies to assess and intervene with depressed young people.

Toolan (1975) has suggested that we seldom see a clear picture of depression in the adolescent. Research regarding the actual incidence of adolescent depression has provided an array of discrepant findings. The range of actual rates varies from as low as 3% of the adolescent population to as high as one-third (Robbins, Alessi, Cook, Poznanski, & Yanchyshyn, 1982). Reynolds (1983) found 34% of a high school student sample to be at least mildly depressed, whereas Albert and Beck (1975) found over a third (36%) of a sample of seventh and eighth grade students to be measurably depressed on the Beck Depression Inventory (Beck, Ward, Mendelson, Mock, & Erbaugh, 1961). Because depression seems either to increase or to become more clinically apparent with age, the trend seems to be increasing rates of adolescent depression with increasing age (McWhirter & Kigin, 1988). Although the reason for this increase is unknown, it is likely due to a multitude of factors.

When a hospitalized adolescent population was evaluated for depression, the percentage of those found to be significantly depressed (major depression) was from 25 to 28% (Carlson & Cantwell, 1982; King & Pittman, 1969; Robbins et al., 1982; Strober, Green, & Carlson, 1981). This is not altogether surprising because, being hospitalized, these young people were already under a great deal of stress. When studies have focused on nonhospitalized adolescents, the reported rates of identifiable depression vary widely, with an average rate of 19% (Albert & Beck, 1975; Kandel & Davies, 1982; Kaplan, Hong, & Weinhold, 1984; Reynolds, 1983; Rutter, Graham, Chadwick, & Yule, 1976). When researchers have investigated age trends and sex differences, the data consistently suggest that females are more prone than males to depression—with the discrepancy in female depression rates manifesting as early as 11 or 12 years of age (Petersen, Sarigiani, & Kennedy, 1991; Robbins & Kashani, 1986).

Masked Depression

When young people experience depression, it may manifest itself more in selected or individualistic symptoms than is the case for adults

(Anthony, 1975). This difference contributes to the belief that children and younger adolescents are immune from full-blown depressive episodes, particularly the pervasive and constant emotional states of sadness and withdrawal and the accompanying motoric symptoms of chronic inertia and sluggishness. Certain writers in the 1970s (e.g., Sheperd, Oppenheim, & Mitchell, 1971) held that the specific developmental behaviors common to younger people overrode the possibility of the more adult-like depressive states. They suggested that both children and adolescents, in times that would normally evoke a depressive response, sometimes behaved quite the opposite, with aggressiveness, hyperactivity, rebelliousness, impulsivity, and acting-out behavior. Such responses were viewed as evidence of *masked depression*, the equivalent of an adult depressive state in children and adolescents. Other symptoms of masked depression might include boredom, excessive tiredness, psychosomatic complaints, and often erratic and very changeable behavior.

In the case that follows, Mark's acting-out behavior is a symptom of masked depression rather than delinquency: Mark, age 14, had been a foster child for 2 years following his father's suicide and his mother's inability to care for him and his three sisters. He was originally placed with a relative after his mother was hospitalized twice for depression and a suicide attempt. But his mother's recovery was slow, and his paternal aunt, whom he was placed with, was too infirm and overwhelmed by her own grief to care well for Mark.

The fact that Mark became truant and was put on probation for a misdemeanor theft charge did not help. After he was arrested for auto theft and resisting arrest, he was referred for psychiatric evaluation. The diagnosis was major depression; the recommendation was for inpatient treatment. The psychiatrist indicated that this was a case of masked depression where multiple losses and change events had precipitated a depressive state that manifested itself in unruly, obstructionist, and rebellious behavior. His report stated that Mark was not a delinquent boy but a grieving and depressed youngster.

Genetic and Family Influences

Is depression inherited? Is suicidal predisposition inherited? These questions, which seem obviously linked, are asked frequently and for good reason. To answer the first question, we must turn to the genetic research related to mood or affective disorders, which include both depression and mania. That literature is typically driven by the *biological causation model*, which states that when one offers a biological intervention such as antidepressant medication, electroshock treatment, or lithium therapy, and there is a measurable change for the better, there must be a biological cause.

The *hereditary hypothesis* suggests that children and adolescents tend to inherit a predisposition toward depression when the parents have been diagnosed as having severe or repetitive depressive episodes (Reich, Rice, & Mullaney, 1986). These findings suggest that children of parents who experience either severe or recurrent depression are more likely than children who do not have depressed parents eventually to develop a depressive disorder. The problem here is in discriminating between the hereditary predisposition and the environmental effects of living with a significant other who manifests depressive behaviors.

The *biochemical dysfunction theory* focuses on possible metabolic alterations and pathologic brain chemistry as causal agents. This position focuses on the destabilization of the neurotransmitters that are essential for appropriate mood and rational thinking. The research in this area, much of it very promising, indicates that there may be a complex interaction among subtle organic factors, heredity, and the environment.

Biological factors may be influential in certain types of depressive states (i.e., major depression and bipolar disorder). The specific mechanisms are not entirely known, nor are the reasons some young people and adults seem more prone than others to such states. The conclusion that biological factors are influential in certain types of depressive states is based on certain fundamental findings summarized by Carson, Butcher, and Coleman (1988):

A predisposition to this type (mood disorders) may be genetically transmitted; the behavioral symptoms of the disorder often abate promptly with certain biological interventions; and certain profound alterations of bodily function, such as changes in the sleep cycle, often accompany the affective symptoms. (p. 297)

In brief, an inherited predisposition to depression appears to exist, but whether that inheritance will prevail depends to some extent on the environment. Living in an unhealthy, neglectful, stressful environment where parents may also model depressive behavior seems to increase the likelihood of an adolescent's experiencing depression.

With respect to the second question, whether suicidal predisposition is inherited, the critical issue concerns the linkage between depressive thinking (ideation) and suicidal behavior. Suicide is *not* inherited, but depression, which can be inherited, does cause ruminative and negative thinking, which in turn causes psychic distress, emotional turmoil, and a desire to terminate that experience. These conditions increase suicide risk.

Concepts of and Approaches to Depression

Behavioral approaches. The behavioral framework has been quite popular in conceptualizing the problems of young people. Essentially, the behavioral approach is derived from the scientific models of learning theory. These models hold that depression will more likely occur when needed social and interpersonal skills are absent. The absence of these skills causes a lack of reinforcement from the environment, which is critical to stable functioning. Depression is seen as resulting from a lack of reinforcement, which creates behavioral and thus emotional deficits. Maher's (1970) theory suggests that a loss event creates a pessimistic attitude that decreases the ability of the adolescent to compensate adequately for the loss. The concomitant response leads to inertia, behavioral deficits, and increased thoughts and feelings of pessimism.

Nasha, a first-year college student, exhibited just such a reaction to the breakup of her first romantic relationship. Dating had always been distressing to her because her older sister was one of the more popular and active girls in high school. But Nasha experienced a whirlwind romance the summer before she entered college. She and her boyfriend Ted had spent every available moment together and eventually experienced their first moments of emotional and physical intimacy. It was painful to part when she left for the state university and Ted remained at home to work and attend the local junior college.

In spite of writing frequently and returning home for many weekends, she noticed a difference in Ted, a slight but certain distance. She felt devastated when her best girlfriend told her that Ted was seeing another girl. Ted admitted this when confronted and said that it was over between him and Nasha. Nasha returned to school but ate little and slept even less. Her college friends unsuccessfully encouraged her to go out with them and accept the date offers of a boy in their coed dormitory. Nasha left school at the end of the term and eventually needed the help of a therapist.

Nasha's troubles are partially explained by the powerful pessimism and the concomitant inactivity that often accompany this type of loss. Perhaps if she had been more experienced and mature in dating and romantic relationships, she would have been able to cope better. As she succumbed to withdrawal and isolation, her world became more narrow and, from a behavioral perspective, the reinforcement necessary to sustain her participation was extinguished. This activity reduction led to further vacancies that precipitated the additional loss of support from Nasha's friends.

If Nasha had been referred to a behaviorally oriented therapist, she might have been strongly encouraged to (a) monitor her mood and behavior to determine the whens and wheres of her negative mood and inactivity (baseline); (b) identify positive substitute activities to counter the behaviors maintaining her pessimistic and apathetic behavior (e.g., attending movies, talking with friends, visiting relatives); (c) set up environmental contingencies that would optimize more pleasant experiences and evoke a more positive mood ("What can you do, where can you go when those feelings begin to occur?"); and (d) contract with the therapist to complete specific assignments to further counteract her tendency to surrender to the effects of pessimism.

Cognitive-behavioral approaches. Although depression is considered primarily a mood disorder, the thinking of a depressed youngster is also typically negative. Aaron Beck and his colleagues at the University of Pennsylvania (Beck et al., 1979) have argued quite persuasively that the negative cognitions of a depressed person can be changed to positive thoughts that will then positively modify the emotional or mood state. Their work, subjected to scientific scrutiny sponsored by the National Institute of Mental Health (Simons, Murphy, Levine, & Wetzel, 1986), has met with much success.

A large group of inpatients who had all been diagnosed with major depression were offered one of three types of treatments: antidepressant medication, cognitive-behavioral therapy, or interpersonal therapy (Klerman, Weissman, & Rounsaville, 1984). The latter two approaches involved brief cognitive-behavioral therapy targeting self-defeating thinking; interpersonal therapy focused on modifying the interpersonal issues influencing or being influenced by the depressive state. Both approaches were found to be as effective as antidepressant medication in alleviating depression, although the nonmedicinal approaches required slightly more time to work effectively.

Generally, the emphasis in cognitive-behavioral treatment is on systematic interruption of obsessive and negative thinking. The theoretical underpinning of this approach is the assumption that feeling is largely a by-product of thinking. The depressed adolescent is educated to determine the nature and frequency of aberrant cognitions (e.g., "I'll never be able to have a boyfriend again," "I'm not lovable," "Life is terrible," "I don't deserve to live") and then to break into that thinking pattern and the underlying attitudes that may have caused and are maintaining the depressive system of thought. Other behavioral tasks, such as assertiveness training, are assigned to reduce behavioral inertia.

A summary of the techniques of this promising approach to depression has been provided by Kaslow and Rehm (1983):

- Educate the client in recognizing the relationship between cognition (thoughts), affect (feelings and mood), and behavior.

- Monitor negative thoughts that have become automatic.

- Confront the irrational evidence that tends to maintain the automatic negative thinking.

- Dispute the negative thinking with a more positive, reality-based interpretation.

- Develop a more consistent productive thinking repertoire that will preclude not only temporary self-defeating thoughts ("I probably won't do well on this exam") but also distorted and pessimistic belief systems ("I'll never be asked to the prom unless I drastically change my appearance").

Much of this work had its roots in the theories of Albert Ellis (1970) and has achieved an impressive record of scientific validation. More research, however, is needed in the area of cognitive-behavioral treatment and intervention with adolescents (Kolko, 1987).

SUMMARY

Adolescents today are confronted by numerous stressors, including breakdown of the family, indifference from institutions, and disregard by the community. The present conditions demand that individuals have the internal and social resources to deal with stress productively. Unfortunately, many adolescents are facing an increasingly stressful world without the positive modeling or support at home or elsewhere to provide them with effective coping mechanisms. Without the tools to cope with the stressors they face, adolescents are often unable to deal with demanding peer relationships, the changes of puberty, death and divorce, and other crises.

The family system, ideally a supportive and enabling environment, is itself in transition and crisis. Certain family characteristics are, in fact, known to increase suicide risk and behavior. These include specific problems in the parent-adolescent relationship, as well as mental health problems and major losses.

In addition, cognitive components of depression, such as pessimism, interact with feelings of hopelessness and worthlessness to create suicidal vulnerability. There is still some debate over whether depressive and suicidal behaviors are inherited or learned. A hereditary predisposition toward depression does seem to exist, but environmental factors play a crucial role in determining whether or not the predisposition will ever emerge. Suicidal behavior per se is not inherited, but the tendency toward depression, which can lead to suicide, is. Suicide risk increases as symptoms of depression worsen. Thus, when signals of depression are noted in young people, psychological assessment and intervention are warranted. Behavioral and cognitive-behavioral interventions with depressed and suicidal adolescents are frequently used. Both approaches have shown promise.

CHAPTER 3

Assessing Suicide Risk

Assessing suicide risk is not a task that comes easily. Asking another human being about his or her intent to live or die is not part of standard conversation. The reasons for not asking are varied, but many professionals believe that reluctance to do so is based on our sensitivity to privacy or the personal threat that accompanies the shock of learning that someone close to us may wish to die. Nevertheless, that inquiry must be made of anyone suspected of being suicidal.

It is a paradox of suicide assessment that the people who know the most about what to look for are often in the least effective position to evaluate. Kirk and Goecken (1983) surveyed both professionals and nonprofessionals regarding their ability to identify signals of suicide and found that psychologists, psychiatrists, and physicians scored significantly higher on an objective 13-item suicide lethality scale than did ministers, lawyers, and laypersons. Scoring dangerously low on the scale were the people most likely to be privy to this type of information—adolescents and their parents. This finding is particularly distressing because suicidal young people often communicate their intent most clearly to their peers. It also underscores the necessity of educating everyone in profiling the suicidal adolescent.

Accurate assessment of suicide risk demands knowledge of factors that may put an adolescent at risk as well as of the symptoms the at-risk adolescent may display. It also requires the clinical or interpersonal skills to communicate with the adolescent in a sensitive but therapeutically firm manner. This chapter will discuss risk factors and signals to look for in conducting a basic suicide assessment.

It is important to note before detailing these risk factors and signals that one of the most essential qualities the assessor can possess when interacting with an at-risk adolescent is a commitment to life. If the assessor is ambivalent about whether or not individuals have the right to take their own lives if they so desire, then that ambivalence may be communicated to the suicidal adolescent. The indecisiveness of the assessor regarding suicide could thus increase the adolescent's self-destructive impulse rather than inhibit it. A firm belief that suicide is an unacceptable option is critical.

RISK FACTORS AND SIGNALS ASSOCIATED WITH SUICIDE

Although suicide signals may manifest themselves differently with each suicidal youngster, certain adolescent behaviors and characteristics are consistently related to increased suicide risk. It is important to note that most of these occur interactively as suicide risk increases. For example, in his review of behavioral characteristics related to prior suicidal behavior, Farberow (1989) found that gradual withdrawal from friends and family was consistently associated with suicidal behavior. Some suicidal adolescents are described as being loners throughout youth (Khan, 1987), but many, over a period of time, detach and disengage from virtually all meaningful support systems. The following behaviors or characteristics, presented in relative order of severity, interrelate as part of an overall constellation of symptoms that correlate with and indicate potential suicidal behavior.

Previous Suicide Attempts

Once an adolescent has demonstrated the willingness and the ability to attempt suicide, he or she remains at higher risk. Indeed, a previous suicide attempt may be the single best predictor of eventual suicide. One of the difficulties in using a previous suicide attempt as an index of prediction is that a family may elect to keep school personnel and even other family members from knowing about the suicide attempt, thus suppressing information that is critical for assessing the adolescent's risk.

Direct or Indirect Communication of Suicidal Intent

The majority of suicidal adolescents attempt to communicate their suicidal intent somehow (Brent et al., 1988). Such communication may not be in the form of a direct statement, but psychological autopsies show that there usually is some indication of the intent of the young person. Such an expression may take many forms.

Verbal Signals

The adolescent may say something direct, like "I'm tired of living," "I wish I were dead," or "Life isn't what it's cracked up to be." These and similar statements typically reflect extreme distress, hopelessness, and feelings of despair.

Written Warnings

Some young people, unable to verbalize their pain, may write poems or notes to friends, parents, or teachers in an attempt to communicate their ambivalence about life and death. The following case demonstrates this point: A recently relocated junior high school student, Raoul, worked hard on an essay for his English class. The essay was about an adolescent who, having recently relocated, was having trouble making friends at school. Finally, Raoul's character kills himself. Raoul turned in the paper, but it wasn't until that evening that his teacher read it. Disturbed, the teacher immediately called the principal of the school, and they agreed to seek counseling for the young man in the morning. But while they were talking, paramedics were trying in vain to revive Raoul, whose sister had found him in his room with a plastic bag over his head. Raoul's method of suicide was identical to that of his fictional character.

A deeply troubled adolescent may leave notes or messages to be found by parents or siblings or, as in the case of Raoul, may insert a disguised message in a homework assignment. A marked preference for books, song lyrics, or films that thematically represent death, suicide, or self-destruction may be present. The importance of reading between the lines and taking even such indirect messages seriously cannot be overstated.

Giving Possessions Away

When an adolescent systematically gives away important possessions, this should be considered a clear signal that he or she is considering self-destruction. Why adolescents begin to divest themselves of their material possessions during the suicide process is not completely understood. The giving away of possessions may be a ritualistic behavior, functioning as a final good-bye and symbolic connection with others.

The friends of one young woman found the following poem under the windshield wiper of her car:

If I share my gifts with you
Please hold them dear, hold them dear
Since I'm feeling kind of blue
Please guess the reason for my fear.
I'll hold our relationship close to me
But four's a crowd—never three.
Don't show my body to everyone
Such changes will occur
That only lovers WHO ARE NONE

Only say things with a slur.
Please divide my tapes equally
and let me go peacefully.
For what in life was hurt and pain
Now becomes something so very sane.
—Ruby

P. S. Give my car to the Community Action Club

When her friends confronted Ruby with the note, she denied her depression. The worried and confused friends reluctantly left her alone, and within the hour she ingested enough prescription medication to kill herself. Luckily, her friends returned in time to save her. The poem provided sufficient information to determine suicidal intent.

Making a Will and/or Arrangements for a Funeral

The gestures of making a will or arranging a funeral seem so melodramatic in adolescents that they are sometimes misinterpreted or dismissed as warped humor. However, when a troubled adolescent begins to plan passage rites, a suicide attempt may follow.

Depression

Previous discussion of depressive episodes and states in young people spelled out the need to recognize depressive symptoms because they are closely related to suicidal thinking and behavior (see chapter 2). A list of the most common symptoms of depression, essential in assessing suicide risk, follows. Any of these symptoms may indicate that there is something wrong in the life of the adolescent.

Hopelessness and Despair

For young people to avoid hopelessness, they must have viable options regarding who they choose to be and what they choose to do. When power and control are taken from them, either suddenly or slowly, adolescents tend to give in to apathy and inertia. Such apathy inhibits their adopting an appropriate role in managing their own lives. Expressions (either verbal or written) of excessive fatigue or being tired of life, school, or any other situation may reflect hopelessness, as may social withdrawal, isolation, fear, timidity, and inhibition.

Helplessness

Helplessness is often the product of an overcontrolling environment in which the adolescent is given little control over his or her life-style, companions, or activities. Helplessness can lead to negative self-esteem, lowered interest in activities, and other depressive features. Seligman (1975) has suggested that feelings or states of helplessness often accompany depression and inhibit active and therapeutic behaviors that would contradict suicidal behavior. Helpless behavior might be situational—that is, a temporary state in which some environmental force is blocking goal-directed behavior. Or helplessness might be a characteristic trait that has been learned in early childhood. The more constant state of helplessness is thought to be most dangerous, although both states are destructive. Feelings of powerlessness and incompetence lead to social withdrawal, the expectation of failure, and, eventually, self-blame.

Worthlessness and Self-Deprecation

As manifested in both hopelessness and helplessness, the depressed adolescent frequently suffers from a constant sense of inadequacy, even if outwardly successful (e.g., the young person gets good grades and has many friends).

Sadness and Morbidity

Most young people experience sadness as a transient mood typically attached to a loss. A depressed adolescent tends to feel sad much of the time and maintains concomitant morbid thoughts. This sadness may be demonstrated through postural problems, slow movement, inattentiveness, or "spaciness." Dwelling on themes of death, dying, and permanent separation is common, and occasionally themes of the desire to be hurt may evolve.

Decreased Attention and Distractibility

As depression continues, an inability to concentrate evolves. This may be manifested in declining school performance and work habits. Nervousness, excitability, and sensitivity to sounds and stimuli may be present, or the affected youth may appear generally preoccupied and inattentive.

Apathy and Inertia

Although they overlap with many other symptoms of depression, apathy and inertia specifically lead to a lack of interest in things that once excited or pleased the adolescent. In addition, a concomitant loss of interest in personal grooming and self-care is not uncommon among adolescents who are depressed.

Eating and Sleeping Disruptions

Impaired ability to eat or sleep is common among depressed youths. In particular, constant early morning awakening can indicate a serious problem—more so than the inability to fall asleep at night. The adolescent becomes reluctant to join the family and friends at mealtimes, often playing with food distractedly. He or she may always seem fatigued, spending time lying in bed or on a sofa, awake and obsessing.

Anxiety and Agitation

Not all depressed and suicidal young people appear anxious or tense, but a constant level of anxiety usually exists when depression develops. The greater the agitation, the more difficult it is for the adolescent to live with his or her symptoms. The unpleasantness of this type of tension and the desire to rid oneself of it may push the young person to act out. This can include self-destructive behaviors ranging from risk taking to direct suicide threats and attempts. Other less extreme manifestations of anxiety include fidgeting, nervousness, distractibility, and a generally high level of physical tension.

Physical Deterioration

Because of the nature of depressive symptoms, the depressed adolescent will usually manifest some physical deterioration. This deterioration may include weight loss, fatigue, decrease in activity and personal hygiene, and frequent complaints of illness.

Multiple and Chronic Stressors

In his groundbreaking work on youth suicide, Jacobs (1971) compared a relatively large group of adolescent suicide attempters with nonsuicidal but psychiatrically disturbed and diagnosed counterparts. He found both similarities and differences. Both groups suffered from traumatic and similar types of problems. They both experienced major and minor family unrest (including alcoholism and divorce), relocations, school problems, losses (including deaths of friends), substance abuse, and, interestingly, high rates of suicides of family members and friends. The significant difference between the two groups was the actual *number* of problems experienced by the suicidal group. The suicidal young people were apparently overwhelmed by the larger number of problems confronting them.

These findings corroborate the pioneering work of Holmes and Rahe (1967) and the more recent efforts of Hawton, O'Grady, Osborne, and Cole (1982), who also found a relationship between duration and number of problems and the seriousness of adolescents' suicide attempts. As the number and duration of stressor events increased, the lethality of the suicide attempts increased.

In brief, as the pressure of long-term multiple stressors builds, thoughts about death, self-destruction, and the act of suicide increase, often to an obsessive level. The interaction of multiple stressors and an adolescent's limited coping repertoire can thus lead to suicidal behavior.

Substance Abuse

Young people who abuse drugs are manifesting their problems with the world blatantly. Not all young people who demonstrate substance abuse are suicidal, but a number of suicidal adolescents also abuse drugs and alcohol (Crumley, 1982). The profile of the suicidal adolescent more often than not includes the frequent use of drugs and alcohol (Shafii et al., 1985). The relationships between substance abuse and suicide are as follows:

- Alcohol and drugs are often used to disinhibit and lower the internal controls of an already distressed and troubled youth.

- When alcohol is used to self-medicate, it stimulates a deeper state of psychophysiological depression as a central nervous system suppressant.

- Overdosing with drugs and alcohol is a common method of suicide used by adolescents (Curran, 1987).

- Parents and other family members of suicidal young people are often addicted to chemicals (McKenry et al., 1983) and therefore provide an unstable home life and model dysfunctional coping for their children. Young people also use their parents' drugs to overdose.

Signs of drug and alcohol abuse include erratic and impulsive acting out or withdrawn and spacey behaviors, depending upon the types of drugs used. Some physical indicators include speech slurring and hoarseness, dilated pupils, sluggish responsivity, and red or swollen eyes.

Conduct Disorders

Antisocial and aggressive behavior has been linked with adolescent suicide attempts (Garfinkel, Froese, & Hood, 1982) and completions (Shaffer & Gould, 1987). Aggressive symptoms may be part of the masked depressive profile discussed in chapter 2. In any event, the risk of suicide must be considered when the adolescent is acting out in a variety of unsocial or antisocial ways.

Conduct disorders may be manifested in classic entanglements with the law and authorities, including shoplifting, stealing, drug dealing, or prostitution. Minor but constant and pervasive conflictual encounters with adults and peers must also be taken into account.

Schizophrenia and Psychotic Disorders

Schizophrenic episodes among the young are not common, but when an adolescent does fall victim to this disorder and begins to experience hallucinations or develop delusions, he or she may become quite vulnerable to suicidal ideation. The case of Tony, as reported by a counselor in a university counseling center, graphically illustrates this point:

> Tony was thought odd by his classmates, but many college freshmen are timid in the beginning. He never did develop friendships or support systems, so when he began to slip into a fantasy world, nobody was there to notice. Eventually Tony deteriorated so much that it came to the notice of the resident assistant in the dormitory, but by then Tony was actively psychotic. We were in the process of contacting his parents and arranging for a major intervention when he attempted to hang himself to "rid himself of the devils" he believed had possessed him. His note was difficult to read but alluded to death as the only escape from his crazy world.

In addition to schizophrenia, the sudden onset of a manic episode, part of bipolar mood disorder (see chapter 2), is considered dangerous due to the impulsivity and irrationality that accompany such a state. The delusions of grandeur and expansive behavior often lead to high-risk behaviors.

An adolescent with schizophrenic/psychotic involvement may demonstrate a gradual deterioration in personal hygiene and otherwise begin to act strangely. Typically, there is a change from previous behaviors, including extreme mood shifts, anxiety and panic episodes, separation anxiety, and reclusiveness. Occasionally, extreme energy bursts that are difficult to understand and manage will signal a manic episode.

Learning Disabilities

Academic deficits and poor attention span may represent personal deterioration and depression. Peck (1986), in performing psychological autopsies of a sample of adolescent suicide deaths, found that half of those victims had some type of diagnosed learning disability. A wide array of possible behaviors an individual may exhibit due to a learning disability exists, but the more common signals are academic problems related to learning and interpersonal problems in relating to peers. Learning disabilities make school adjustment very difficult for affected young people.

TECHNIQUES FOR ASSESSING SUICIDE RISK

Accurate assessment of suicide risk demands knowledge about signals and symptoms such as the ones just discussed, as well as the clinical or interpersonal skills to communicate with a suicidal adolescent in a sensitive but therapeutically firm manner. The following discussion makes some recommendations for assessing and interacting with a young person suspected of harboring suicidal thoughts or planning a suicidal act.

Formal Suicide Assessment

There are two kinds of formal suicide evaluation: consultation by a trained professional and testing involving the use of a validated screening instrument.

Professional Consultation

A parent or friend of a suicidal adolescent may recognize troubling signals and seek the counsel of a teacher, mental health professional, or even another friend. Eventual consultation with a professional trained to assess suicide potential is advisable. Here the physician, mental health professional, or pupil personnel specialist (i.e., school psychologist, social worker, or counselor) can make a more discriminating decision about the immediacy of the crisis and the need to obtain additional assistance.

Various specialists employed by school systems are academically and clinically trained to consult with teachers and students. Guidance counselors, school psychologists, and school social workers have skills in the assessment and treatment of depressed and suicidal youth. Guidance counselors are certified school personnel holding at least a master's degree. Their training focuses on counseling interventions, group and individual assessment, and vocational appraisal. A counselor may specialize in elementary, junior high, or high school level work. The school guidance counselor is specifically trained in addressing personal/emotional issues, which include depression and suicidal behavior.

School psychologists typically hold a master's or education specialist's degree in school psychology. This academic training plus a 1-year internship prepares the school psychologist as a specialist in the assessment and appraisal of psychoeducational and personal problems. The training in both psychological testing and interviewing make the school psychologist an ideal consultant in the assessment of suicidal risk.

School social workers hold a master's of social work degree with a specialization in social work theory and psychosocial intervention. The academic training and requisite field work in schools prepares the social worker to assess family influences on a suicidal adolescent. Many school social workers are trained in counseling methods effective with depressed and suicidal youth.

These specialists' expertise also provides for optimal referral potential to outside agencies or therapists. The effective consultant knows what adolescent to refer, to whom, when, and for what problems. Table 3.1 lists typical referral sources.

Testing

There have been two fairly recent and in-depth reviews of instruments designed to assess childhood and adolescent depression and

Table 3.1 Professional Referral Sources for Suicide Assessment

Schools	School guidance department (counselors)
	Pupil personnel office (school psychologists)
	Social service office (school social workers)
	School nursing office (school nurses)
Mental health agencies	Psychiatrists
	Psychologists
	Social workers
	Counselors
Private sources	Family physicians
	Medical clinics
	Emergency room services
	Psychiatric hospitals and psychiatric units in general hospitals
Suicide services	Crisis telephone services
	Suicide prevention services (often listed in telephone books under suicide, mental health, and/or human services)

suicide potential (Costello & Angold, 1988; Lewinsohn, Garrison, Langhinrichsen, and Marsteller, 1989). These reviewers conclude that currently published measures have more research value than clinical utility (Berman & Jobes, 1991). Plainly, no paper-and-pencil test can ever substitute for the assessment that can and should take place between the suicidal youth and a qualified professional. Fencik (1986), writing in the teacher's manual published by the Samaritans, a national group devoted to preventing suicide, is quite blunt about this point: "There is not a reliable psychological test that will [always] identify someone who is suicidal" (p. 23).

The question of the validity of these tests is appropriate, particularly when the purpose of the instruments—to assess death potential—is considered. Despite the limitations of tests, researchers acknowledge that such tools are useful, even if in a limited capacity (Davis, Sandoval, & Wilson, 1988). The following types of instruments are helpful in the screening of suicidal youth and perhaps can be effective in differentially diagnosing levels of depression or lethality potential.

Tests assessing suicide potential. Certain instruments helpful in assessing suicide potential that are used only by trained professionals are the Suicidal Ideation Questionnaire by Reynolds (1987) and the Suicide Probability Scale by Cull and Gill (1982).

Tests assessing adolescent depression. Tests to evaluate depressive states and symptoms can be particularly effective in assessing for potential suicidal ideation and behavior. The Beck Depression Checklist (Beck et al., 1961) is often used and has been found to be quite reliable in the assessment of levels of depression. Reynolds's Suicidal Ideation Questionnaire (1987) specifically targets the symptoms of depression in a young population. The use of either of these instruments in screening may lead to the identification of high-risk adolescents and thus to effective prevention measures.

Kirk and Davidson (1989) assessed a number of college students to determine the impact of a made-for-television movie graphically portraying a completed double suicide. After the assessment, we were able to screen a number of first-year students for levels of depression and refer those in need of further treatment and counseling. In one case, we immediately intervened with a student who was judged quite depressed on the basis of both the Reynolds and Beck instruments. The student admitted to harboring very serious thoughts of self-destruction. The decision to intervene was made easier when responses on the Suicide Acceptability Scale (Hoelter, 1979) indicated that the student felt suicide was a relatively acceptable option in the face of problems. In

this case, the formal screening procedure, which was originally conducted for the purpose of suicide research, may have been life saving
for this particular at-risk student.

Informal Suicide Assessment

Implementing a suicide assessment is both science and art. The science
derives from knowing what to look for and how to ask the right questions. The professional intervenor has been trained in the science of
suicide assessment. But the individual assessing suicide risk must also
be able to elicit enough information from the troubled youth to determine whether suicide risk exists. This is the art of suicide assessment—
the interpersonal skill of the individual relating to a suicidal adolescent
intuitively, empathically, and constructively. In an informal suicide assessment, the nonprofessional intervenor must rely on these skills. The
goal of such an assessment is to determine whether or not suicide risk
does exist so that, if the situation warrants, referral to a professional
can be made.

Intuition

Intuition is nothing more than our ability to decipher signals in the
environment. Using intuitive skills requires the intelligent use of our
senses. When we translate these skills into suicide assessment, we attempt to decode all of the verbal and nonverbal signals that the young
person is presenting. Table 3.2 offers examples of both verbal and nonverbal statements of suicidal adolescents. The quoted statements are
not literal; rather, they represent internal statements suicidal youths
often make to themselves.

Empathy

Empathy and sympathy have often been confused. The sympa-
thetic listener will feel sorry for the unhappy individual. However, pity
is of little use to someone in psychological pain and may lead to emotional responses in the listener that would block effective assessment.
Empathy requires that the listener work hard at "reading"—inter-
preting and understanding—what is being said and then reflecting this
content back to the individual. The importance of empathy as a core
ingredient in the therapeutic process has been well documented
(Luborsky, Singer, & Luborsky, 1975). The research suggests that the
ability to understand another individual and to communicate that understanding directly and sensitively can have therapeutic and healing
effects.

Table 3.2 Verbal and Nonverbal Statements Indicating Suicide Risk

	Verbal statements	Nonverbal statements
Despair	I want to die. I'm hopeless and helpless.	Motoric sluggishness, physical apathy; withdrawal, isolation
Substance abuse	I'm out of control. I want help but don't know how to use it.	Frequent alcohol and drug consumption
Masked depression	Nothing's wrong that I can't fix by being rebellious and antisocial.	Physical aggression and acting out; anxiety, rebelliousness
Ambivalence	I'm not sure if I want to live or die.	Possible depressive or masked depressive symptoms with some anxiety
Psychic pain	Life is so unbearable, I can't cope with it.	Depressive symptoms combined with anxiety and agitation
Suicidal ideation	Nothing is working. Maybe death is the only way out.	Confusion, despair, ambivalence; increased withdrawal
Suicide plan	One way out is to plan my own death.	Polarized behavior such as separation anxiety, isolation, and withdrawal; agitation; occasionally, tranquility

Because empathy articulates understanding, a self-destructive youngster may feel more comfortable verbalizing his or her feelings to an empathic listener. The expression of understanding from another person will ideally decrease the strength of the adolescent's suicidal impulses. The following exchange between Jim and his school principal provides a good example of empathic listening and paraphrasing.

Jim: I don't want your help. I don't want to be here. Mrs. _____ didn't have any right to make me come.

Principal: Hm, I understand how difficult this must be for you, but she was concerned about you. I'm concerned as well.

Jim: I don't believe that! Nobody is concerned. Why all of a sudden? Nobody cared before.

Principal: That must be a pretty lonely feeling, Jim. How long have you been feeling that way?

Jim: I don't know. *(Puts his head down and begins to cry quietly.)* I'm just so confused.

The principal might have wanted to convince Jim of her desire to help him—it is easy to understand that impulse—particularly when Jim initially presents himself argumentatively. But by remaining objective and working toward understanding Jim's hurt and confusion and only then reflecting her own interpretation, the principal helps Jim reduce his defensiveness and focus on the issues causing his discomfort—loneliness and emotional confusion.

In brief, in offering empathy to another, it is important to do the following: listen to both the verbal and nonverbal messages that the person is sending, offer an interpretation of the person's feelings and thoughts every so often as an accuracy check, and phrase your statements warmly and genuinely.

Methods of Obtaining Information

Indirect methods. There are times when information about a suicidal youth may be gained secondhand. It is important for any assessor to validate that information as quickly and discreetly as possible.

The case of Joan, a high school student, illustrates this point: One day, Joan suddenly and unexpectedly ran from the school cafeteria, leaving an uneaten lunch and a neatly folded poem on her tray. The students she had been sitting with read the poem, which alluded to the "glory of heaven and pains of the earthbound sufferers." They made an appointment with the school psychologist because one of them knew the psychologist as a neighbor and felt relatively comfortable asking her questions about Joan. The psychologist quickly contacted Joan's teachers and discovered that Joan had been acting strangely, missing classes and assignments, then giving her teachers unusual excuses. The school counselor and psychologist then contacted Joan's mother, who was unaware of Joan's problems at school. When they tactfully confronted Joan, she broke down crying and admitted to feeling very suicidal. Her mother later found a notebook of Joan's dedicated to poetry with death themes.

When there is sufficient evidence that an adolescent may be suicidal, the validation process must occur quickly. The ultimate task is to confront the adolescent with the facts in a caring manner. In the case just discussed, Joan's attempt to connect with teachers and friends was so disguised that they were missing her important signals. Fortunately, Joan's desperation led her to be more dramatic about her dilemma. She received intensive individual treatment, and the family entered family therapy. These interventions alleviated Joan's silent suffering and helped her begin to heal.

Direct methods. When suicide is suspected, it is not always an easy task to ask directly whether the individual wants to die. However, if something seems to be troubling an adolescent or if something is significantly wrong or different in his or her academic or social performance, a direct approach is necessary. The inquiry must attempt to gauge risk level by answering the following basic questions:

- Does the adolescent want to die or attempt suicide?

- Does the adolescent have a suicide plan?

- Does the adolescent have the means available to attempt or complete the act?

In writing about assessing suicidal adolescents in the school setting, McBrien (1983) suggests that the assessment process revolves around 10 basic questions. The answers to these questions then serve as a basis for action. McBrien also emphasizes that clinical judgment is critical and urges that the assessor of suicide potential rely strongly on active listening skills and empathic understanding.

1. How much does the student want to die?

2. How much does the student want to live?

3. What are the specifics of any plan that might exist?

4. How often does the student have suicidal thoughts?

5. How long has the student had suicidal thoughts?

6. Has the student made previous suicide attempts?

7. Is there a lifeline to stop the student?

8. Has the student made final arrangements for death or chosen a time to die?

9. What is the chance that the student will kill himself or herself?

10. Why does the student want to die? (p. 80)

The following abstract of the interview with Joan highlights how suicide risk can be assessed directly: After Joan's problems were identified, the school psychologist and counselor called Joan's mother to ask if they could come over to the house and chat with her and Joan about certain concerns they had. Joan's mother disclosed that she had noticed changes in Joan's behavior but couldn't seem to get Joan to tell her if anything was wrong. The psychologist and counselor called a school social worker assigned to the district. They asked the social worker to take Joan out of school early and drive her home, where they would all meet and further evaluate her suicide potential.

> Mother: *(After hugging her daughter)* Joanie, I'm sorry we had to pull you out of school, but Mrs. _____ and Mr. _____ called me about some things I didn't know about.

> Joan: *(Starts to shake and back away.)* What's this all about? Just because I ran out of the stupid lunchroom ... am I in trouble or something? *(Begins to cry.)*

> Counselor: Joan, we're concerned about some things that have been happening at school. We're concerned about you and how you've been feeling.

> Psychologist: Why don't we all have a seat and discuss this? We're all concerned about you, Joan, and we just want to let you know that first and then see if there's a way we can help.

> Mother: *(Puts her arm around Joan's shoulder and moves her toward the living room, where they all take seats. The counselor shares the sofa with Joan and her mother.)* It's OK, honey, it's OK.

> Joan: *(Cries softly.)* I'm in trouble, aren't I?

> Psychologist: No, Joan, but we're wondering what might be going on with you. We didn't know you were missing so many classes, and then when you ran out of the cafeteria today, Alice and Michael came to me because they're concerned about you, too.

> Joan: I knew it ... they snitched. *(Cries.)*

Mother: No, no ... they're your friends, Joanie.

Counselor: Joan, they shared a note with Mr. _____, which was what alarmed us particularly. I'd like it if you would share with us how you're feeling. It sounds to us like you've been pretty upset about some things, and we just want to help.

Joan: *(Begins to cry in spasms.)* This isn't fair! I hate everything! I hate life! *(Leans into her mother.)*

Psychologist: You sound like you're feeling pretty miserable, Joan. How long have you been hurting like this?

Joan: I don't know. *(Gasping)* You're right, though. It hurts. It just hurts so bad.

Mother: Oh God, why didn't you let me know, Joanie?

Joan: Why? Nobody really seemed to care ... nobody.

Mother: *(Looks helplessly at the counselor and psychologist.)*

Psychologist: Joan, one of the things that we're most concerned about is the note you left on the tray. In it you talk about death. Have you been thinking of hurting yourself?

Joan: *(Putting her head in her hands and trying to compose herself, then looking straight at the psychologist)* What makes you think that?

Psychologist: *(Softly)* It wouldn't surprise us, any of us, if that were the case. Considering how bad you're feeling ...

Joan: *(After a long pause, gazing out the window)* Yeah, I've thought about it ... I've thought about suicide. There were times when I really wanted to do it, but I guess I didn't have the guts.

Counselor: *(Placing her hand on Joan's)* We had a hunch that you might be feeling pretty bad, Joan. We just didn't know how bad. *(Pausing and keeping her hand on Joan's, speaking softly and slowly)* Joan, when you thought of hurting yourself, did you feel like you wanted to die?

Joan: I don't know. *(Crying softly again)* I just wanted the hurt to end. I think, maybe, I did ... I just don't know.

> Counselor: We want to help you with that hurt now, Joan. We can do that, but we all need your help. I'm so relieved that we know just how bad you felt.
>
> Mother: *(Breaks down and begins to sob.)*
>
> Joan: *(Puts her arm around her mother. They embrace.)* It's OK, Mom, I'll be all right. I love you.

At this point an open discussion of Joan's condition ensued. With gentle questioning, Joan proceeded gradually to share how she couldn't seem to manage all the pressures of schoolwork and cheerleading combined with the emotional pain of her breakup with her boyfriend the previous summer, which she still felt very keenly. Gradually, she had begun to feel more and more helpless and inadequate.

As Joan disclosed how, harboring her emotional turmoil, she had gradually withdrawn, the counselor, psychologist, and social worker were able to reassure both Joan and her mother that help was available and that no matter what happened from that point on, Joan's life was paramount and her suicide was an unacceptable option. This was communicated gently, with Joan agreeing that suicide was not the answer.

Joan's mother asked about the next step, and the group explored the alternatives. The professional team offered the possibility of referral for hospitalization, which Joan rejected. After a thorough discussion to determine Joan's safety as an outpatient, immediate outpatient treatment was arranged. The counselor drove Joan and her mother to the clinic, and arrangements for communication among Joan, the school counselor, and the psychologist were made.

As this case example suggests, it is extremely difficult for a troubled adolescent to deal adequately with confusion, misery, and unhappiness. As depression envelops the vulnerable youngster, increasing lethargy, discouragement, and concomitant feelings of hopelessness decrease the adolescent's ability to come forward and ask for help directly. The motivation to seek assistance may remain, but the suicidal adolescent may seek refuge in drugs, damaging relationships, further withdrawal, and, eventually, if his or her plight is not recognized and interrupted, suicidal plans and action.

Constructive Confrontation

Once the assessor senses that the adolescent may be having suicidal thoughts, then communicates that understanding empathically, it is important that he or she constructively confront the issue. The principal in Marcus's case illustrates how this may be done.

Principal: *(Gently and warmly)* I sense a lot of turmoil, a lot of pain, Marcus. I'd like you to tell me about it.

Marcus: *(Chokes back tears.)*

Principal: *(After waiting and sensing Marcus's awkwardness)* Marcus, it's OK to cry. It's natural when you're feeling this way.

Marcus: I don't know ... I just don't know anymore. It's all been piling up and ... I'm nothing. Nothing is working. I just don't see any reason for anything anymore. I hate school. I hate everything.

Principal: Tell me about your anger and hate.

Marcus: It's not even that anymore. Maybe that's why I'm so confused. There's just so many things—so many feelings. It always ends up being emptiness ... and nothingness.

Principal: Emptiness ...

Marcus: A dead end ... nowhere.

Principal: Marcus, you're really down, aren't you?

Marcus: *(Haltingly)* Yeah, I guess.

Principal: Marcus, I'm wondering if you've been thinking of some way to stop your hurt?

Marcus: *(Looks directly at the principal and begins to cry again. Bows his head and nods.)*

Principal: *(Positioning herself closer to Marcus)* With all of that inside you, Marcus, my guess is that you've thought of hurting yourself in some way.

Marcus: *(Nods again and begins to sob.)*

Confronting a suicidal youth with the reality of his or her suicidal ambivalence often results in a measure of relief and respite from that misery. Using her ability to empathize and understand, the principal in this case moved to confront Marcus with her intuitions based on how the student presented himself. Such an encounter ideally helps a youngster express how all of his or her experiences, perceptions, and feelings have led to the consideration of death as a means of coping.

The Assessment Interview: Asking the Right Questions in the Right Way

As previously discussed, when an adolescent is suspected of harboring suicidal thoughts, action should be taken immediately. In the school setting, the intervenor will first need to consult with another educator or the administrator to confirm the suicide risk. Once the risk has been confirmed, the intervenor should, of course, consult a qualified professional who will help assess the degree of risk and identify the broadest range of interventions possible.

In conducting an assessment interview, it is imperative to communicate a basic message of care and concern to provide a background for the more specific suicide inquiry. The necessity of establishing a positive working relationship with the young person is critical to making a timely determination of risk. Table 3.3 lists some statements and questions that can be used to facilitate positive contact with the adolescent.

The following questions are also offered as guides to help the assessor. Not in any special order, these questions are listed under three separate categories: thoughts, feelings, and behaviors.

Thoughts

- Do any thoughts about suicide exist?
- What specifically are those thoughts?
- How serious do those thoughts appear to be?
- Are they specific or ambiguous?
- Is there a specific plan related to the suicidal thoughts?
- If a plan exists, what are the thoughts about how the adolescent would carry out the plan?
- Are the means to carry out the plan available?

Essentially, the thoughts of the suicidal adolescent tend to focus on themes of death, ambivalence, and escape from a situation he or she perceives as intolerable.

Feelings

- Are there feelings of hopelessness? If so, how severe are these feelings?
- Do feelings of worthlessness exist? If so, how extensive are these feelings?

Table 3.3 Statements and Questions Facilitating Positive Contact

Do	How to say it
Establish and maintain rapport	Chris, I've been wondering ... Mary, I've been concerned lately ... Carlos, how have you been doing lately? It seems that ...
Communicate sincerity and genuineness	I want you to know I care about ... Daphene, the reason I'm asking is because I want to help ...
Be willing to address the real issue	Have you been thinking about ... You've seemed so _____, so I was wondering if you wanted to do anything to hurt yourself.
Take action; don't leave the adolescent alone	Malcolm, I'm going to call Ms. _____ so the three of us can talk about ... Rita, let's walk down to ...
Reinforce the adolescent's willingness to open up	I'm so glad you've shared your feelings with me ... It's really important to me that you're open about this, Holly.
Communicate a sense of therapeutic teamwork	You won't be alone during this, Michelle. Robert, we'll help you through this.

- Is there a level of helplessness? If so, how helpless does the adolescent feel?

- Does the adolescent have feelings of discouragement and despair? If so, at what level do these feelings exist?

- Are there feelings of anger or resentment that might be causing the adolescent to act out suicidally?

- Is there a level of emotional confusion that might be interfering with the ability of the adolescent to think rationally about life?

The suicidal adolescent may present with the affective triad of hopelessness, helplessness, and worthlessness. Confusion, bewilderment, and anger are also common.

Behaviors

- Has the adolescent withdrawn and become isolated?

- Is there any evidence of acting out or indication of masked depression?

- Are there any direct signals of making plans for death, such as giving things away or making a will?

- Have any indirect signals been observed, such as playing with weapons, making subtle statements about being tired of life, going to cemeteries, or asking questions about where one can acquire medication or a weapon?

- Do any signals of erratic, impulsive, or unusual behavior exist?

- Are there any observable signals of depression, such as motoric sluggishness or excessive fatigue?

- Are extreme and sudden mood shifts apparent?

- Is there evidence of chronic substance abuse or any indication of a significant shift to or from alcohol or drug abuse?

The behavioral indicators that need to be assessed generally involve changes. Those changes may be found in global behavior, personality functioning, academic performance, social functioning, or health status. In some cases these changes are subtle or develop over a long time. If a friend, relative, or teacher notices long-term deterioration or sudden changes, he or she should consult with someone else to validate those observations and attempt to explain the reasons for them. Consultation with a professional is then advisable.

SUMMARY

This chapter has presented some of the risk factors and signals associated with adolescent suicide and has explored assessment techniques. Risk factors and signals of suicidal intent include previous suicide attempts, direct or indirect communication of suicidal intent, depression, multiple and chronic stressors, substance abuse, conduct disorders, schizophrenia and psychotic disorders, and learning disabilities.

If an adolescent is experiencing suicidal ideation, immediate assessment is recommended. Professional assessment through either interviews, tests, or both is always beneficial. However, in the case of suspicions that have not yet been validated, the nonprofessional can employ certain techniques to determine whether or not the adolescent is, in fact, suicidal. Such techniques include using intuition, talking to the adolescent empathically, and using constructive confrontation.

The assessment interview is an easily employed technique to determine suicide risk, with questions focusing on three realms: the adolescent's thoughts, feelings, and behaviors. If the assessment interview reveals that any level of suicidal ideation does exist, referral to a qualified professional is necessary.

CHAPTER 4

Intervention Strategies

This chapter discusses intervention strategies for interrupting the suicide process in an adolescent identified as at risk. A brief discussion of levels of suicide risk precedes an examination of general crisis intervention strategies. The nature and stages of crisis are next discussed, and steps for intervening in a crisis situation are presented. Finally, procedural suggestions for intervention in the school setting are offered.

LEVELS OF SUICIDE RISK

Risk level affects how the intervenor approaches the adolescent and determines the content and procedures involved in intervention. Inasmuch as both the high-risk and low-risk individual are expressing a wish to die, they both must be taken seriously. However, an adolescent at low-risk may benefit from regular sessions with a school counselor, psychologist, or social worker who is in consultation with an outside professional. The high-risk student may require the more extreme measure of hospitalization to prevent completion of the act.

In general, risk is a function of suicidal ideation, concrete planning, and availability of means. When suicidal ideation culminates in some level of concrete planning, suicide risk increases. If the means to implement the plan are also available, the risk becomes even greater. However, suicidal behavior is not always predictable, and it is dangerous to assume that intervention may be terminated if a plan exists without specific means. For example, Ann, a 15-year-old inpatient at a psychiatric hospital, had admitted to having some fantasies about being dead. However, when staff assessed for a suicide plan Ann always indicated that she didn't know how she would take her own life. The staff believed her and thought she was only mildly at risk. They learned better when they caught her actually attempting suicide.

In addition, the planning sequence for suicide is often very unsystematic. An adolescent might have fantasies about how, when, and where the suicide would occur but not have an identifiable means immediately available. However, when such a young person encounters additional pain or trauma, he or she could easily convert those fantasies into concrete behavior and become high risk very quickly. In brief, the rapidly shifting, unpredictable emotions of the suicidal adolescent, especially when combined with the viability and availability of suicide means, make it extremely dangerous to delay consultation with a professional once suicidal ideation has been observed.

It is also important to stress that an intervenor's feeling that a student is at moderate or low risk is no guarantee that this is actually the case. Risk levels are mere guidelines, and it is always better to err on the side of safety. However, the concept of risk level is a useful tool in tailoring intervention strategies to meet the needs of a specific adolescent. As long as the intervenor keeps in mind the changeable nature of risk level, a risk assessment can provide a starting point for intervention efforts.

High Risk

Adolescents at high risk typically meet the following criteria:

- They have feelings and thoughts about killing themselves immediately or in the near future.

- They tend to have a specific, irreversible plan for completing the act and possess the means by which to complete it.

- They harbor certain symptoms of depression or agitation, some of which may be more readily identifiable than others.

A history of previous suicide attempts or gestures also indicates high risk. Whatever the history, when high suicide risk is determined, intervention by a qualified professional—including possible hospitalization—must be made immediately.

Moderate Risk

Moderate risk for suicide exists when an individual currently has or has had thoughts of suicide but does not feel frightened of acting on those thoughts immediately. A specific or detailed plan for suicide does not exist, and the means of carrying out the suicide are not immediately available. Although a moderate-risk adolescent probably does not have a history of previous suicide attempts or gestures, he or she may have a history of suicidal ideation.

Intervention with a moderate-risk adolescent is similar to that for the high-risk adolescent, although less immediate implications may exist for emergency procedures. Referral to counseling is necessary, but such referral may be to a specialist within the school, such as a counselor, psychologist, or social worker. This specialist may need to consult with another professional regarding the best course of action to take.

Low Risk

An individual assessed at low risk for suicide potential generally meets the following criteria:

- There is no history of suicide attempts or gestures, but there is or has been some level of suicidal ideation.

- There is no current motivation to die, but some symptoms related to presuicide status may exist (minimal or moderate depression, discouragement, or distress).

- There are no definite or current plans or means available.

Counseling in the school setting is important for the low-risk student, with referral to an outside source taking place if the risk level increases.

When suicide risk of any level is determined within the school environment, a decision must be made about alerting parents or guardians. This is typically done after an assessment is complete and school personnel have some idea of the student's risk level. Different mental health codes and school policies govern how and when parents must be informed of the mental health status of their children.

GENERAL INTERVENTION STRATEGIES

As soon as an assessment suggests that a youth is experiencing suicidal ideation (see chapter 3), intervention becomes necessary. Although the help of a professional is essential if suicide risk exists, any individual who becomes privy to the suicidal signals of an adolescent is in a critical position to intervene. The general guidelines for intervention next discussed are intended not to replace the care of a trained professional but to precede or supplement it.

The Intervenor's Attitudes and Beliefs

The effective intervenor in any context maintains attitudes and beliefs that are as important as his or her technical skills. Both play a role in successful suicide intervention. The following attitudes and beliefs are central because, without them, the intervenor may be influenced by antitherapeutic personal issues or be indecisive in the effort to help.

The effective intervenor believes that suicide is an unacceptable option for the adolescent. In order to avoid sending the adolescent a subtle or unconscious message about the acceptability of self-destruction, the intervenor must be totally committed to life as the only option.

The effective intervenor recognizes that the suicidal adolescent is experiencing a failure of adaptation and can be helped over time to acquire productive coping and healthy living skills. Suicide is often a process of gradual decline in coping specifically influenced by internal pressures and external events. The majority of adolescents who experience effective intervention adapt and renew their appreciation for life.

The effective intervenor makes a commitment to the suicidal adolescent by acknowledging personal limitations and by making use of all possible resources to optimize the individual's life potential. The instigation of broad support is essential to the adolescent. It is important to realize the potential pitfalls of attempting intervention without the help of others, both nonprofessionals and professionals. Levels of stress, time limitations, the personal relationship, and negative feelings toward the adolescent may all inhibit the intervenor's total effectiveness. Professional consultation provides the intervenor the opportunity to develop critical insights into his or her clinical decision making and to assess any perceptual blind spots that may inhibit life-saving efforts.

The effective intervenor has or is willing to develop an information base and skills in assessment of and intervention with suicidal adolescents. The information and skills need periodic updating to enable the intervenor to remain personally and clinically proficient.

The following case illustrates the trouble an intervenor can cause by not acknowledging personal limitations—specifically, by not maintaining the proper level of emotional detachment: Sean, a high-school senior, was filled with all the hopes and expectations typical of a college-bound student. Then an accident involving Sean and his best friend, Eddy, changed all that. The car Sean was driving was hit by another vehicle, and Eddy was killed. The accident was judged to be the other driver's fault, but Sean couldn't shake the feeling that if he had done something differently, Eddy would be alive. He could no longer concentrate on his schoolwork and became obsessed with thoughts about death.

Sean's family and friends tried to console and support him, with little effect. Their family physician said that the psychological wounds would take at least a year to heal and suggested that Sean see the guidance counselor at school. Sean decided to take this advice.

Unfortunately, the counselor at school was Eddy's cousin. At first, the therapeutic relationship seemed to work out. During biweekly counseling sessions both Sean and the counselor felt and shared their mutual grief and pain. During these meetings Sean felt that his grief was understood. The feeling of companionship relieved him for a short while after his sessions. But too soon, the heaviness and despair would return to haunt him. It was less than a year after Eddy's death that Sean hanged himself from a tree close to the spot where the accident occurred.

The task of the suicide intervenor is to bring all available personal and professional resources to bear in identifying the level of suicide risk and interrupting the suicide process. In this case the counselor's own psychological status impaired his ability to intervene effectively. Although he thought he was providing Sean an empathic arena, he was in fact dealing with his own personal response to his cousin's death instead of attending fully to his client. By consoling his grief-stricken client with his own disclosures and unresolved grief, he gave Sean an additional burden. Had the counselor realized his limitations and consulted with another professional when Sean came to him, in all probability Sean would have been referred to a different therapist. The outcome might have been different.

Guidelines for Intervention

In addition to maintaining appropriate attitudes and beliefs, the intervenor can employ certain practical techniques to facilitate the intervention process. The following guidelines suggest technical and procedural steps that should be followed in order to assure adequate intervention.

Be Available and Accessible

Making oneself available and accessible psychologically and physically may sound simplistic, but doing so is an important component of the suicide intervention process.

Psychological accessibility. When a young person is in the throes of a life-and-death struggle, he or she is typically looking for a lifeline. A teacher, parent, friend, or clinician who is available, interested, and nonjudgmental is more likely to be acceptable as that lifeline.

Although students may not be able to articulate exactly why they finally turn to one person over another, on some level they understand who is psychologically accessible to them. The following quote from a suicidal 16-year-old illustrates this point:

> I went to my history teacher because she seemed to be there—she was always there. I always admired the way she wanted to help any of us who were having difficulties with assignments, but it went beyond that. I don't know for sure how to describe it. All the other teachers and even the counselor seemed to be so hassled all the time.

Physical accessibility. To help an adolescent with a conflict or difficulty one must be physically available for meaningful contact. It is important for the helper to communicate that availability to the suicidal adolescent. The intervenor should make clear when and where he or she can be located and stress that students are always welcome to stop in and talk. Suicidal adolescents turn to those whom they trust and can find.

> It was strange how I ended up at our neighbors. I was in a daze walking home from school that day. I just knocked on the door, and when she answered I started to cry. I knew she would be there just like she always was for her own kids.

Obviously, "being there" for suicidal adolescents is an impression that the intervenor must develop over time. However, consistent availability, reliability, interest, and empathy will eventually increase the chances that a disturbed adolescent will turn to the intervenor.

Make Therapeutic Contact and Establish Rapport

When clues or signals of the suicide process are observed, the intervenor must gain access to the psychological world of the troubled adolescent. Establishing therapeutic contact is a critical step in creating an environment in which the adolescent will feel free to discuss feelings of despair, hopelessness, and panic. This demands communicating a caring, confident, and competent attitude—the three C's of therapeutic contact.

A caring attitude. Statements that tend to facilitate this might include "I'm concerned. I do care about you. It's important to me that you know I care and that's why I . . ."

A confident attitude. Projecting a confident attitude has a calming effect on the adolescent. The intervenor may not be a professional and thus may not know all of the technical issues related to suicide intervention, but he or she needs to be confident of being able to support the adolescent until other professional help can be obtained. The world of the suicidal adolescent is a world of turmoil and confusion, and the adolescent in this state usually needs to reestablish psychological organization and order. These derive, in part, from the helper's degree of confidence.

A competent attitude. Establishing competence is much like communicating confidence. Competence suggests to the adolescent that the intended helper is aware of what is happening (or wants to find out) and knows what to do about it. The adolescent very likely will not communicate his or her intentions or feelings to someone who cannot or does not communicate competence.

Assess for Imminence

When a troubled youth is assessed for suicide, the assessment generally results from one of two indicators: (a) the adolescent's indirect or direct contact with another person in the form of a plea for help or (b) recognition of certain suicidal signals by someone relatively close to the adolescent. When either of these situations presents itself, certain basic efforts need to be undertaken immediately to evaluate the potential lethality, or imminence, of suicide.

In most cases, evaluations of imminence involve an interview to assess for suicide intent, plan, and method. This assessment gives the intervenor the basic information regarding immediacy and risk level required to institute treatment.

Evaluate for suicide intent. The assessment of intent involves a therapeutic inquiry into the motives of the suicidal adolescent. Questions such as "Do you want to hurt yourself or harm yourself" may help to broach the subject of self-destruction. Eventually, however, the question "Do you want to die or kill yourself" must be asked.

Evaluate for possible plan. Determining whether a suicidal adolescent has a plan to die is best done by asking simple questions such as "Now that I know you feel this way, I'd like to know how you would injure (or kill) yourself." Some inquiry about the specificity of the plan is always in order. If the adolescent has set a particular time for the suicide, for instance, the lethality index would be considered very high.

Evaluate for possible method. Generally, the more concrete the suicide plan, the more likely it is that the adolescent will have access to some means of completing the act. Questions that attempt to determine method are typically forthright and direct: "Do you have a gun? Do you know how to use it?" or "Are there pills in your home? What kind of pills are you talking about?" The intervenor should be as specific as necessary to ascertain complete information about the plan and the means of self-destruction. Any error of omission at this point could have tragic consequences.

The following example illustrates the consequences of an inadequate evaluation of imminence: A mental health counselor was working with a troubled young man referred for school problems, including suspected substance abuse. This high school freshman was 2 years older than his peers, having been retained twice in earlier grades. The counselor wisely assessed for suicide after the student made a reference to being "tired of it all." The counselor judged the student to be at low to moderate risk after he indicated a desire to be dead but was vague about how he would kill himself. Two days later, after being suspended from school for fighting, the student drank 12 beers and died after he drove his motorcycle at high speed into an oncoming truck. His parents found a set of rambling notes about how cruel and unfair life was.

If the counselor's assessment had been more comprehensive, particularly during the evaluation of intent, a different outcome might have resulted. Some individuals can be highly lethal, particularly when responding to the impact of a sudden precipitant or stressor, even when a suicide plan is vague or nonexistent. Whenever the motivation to die is present, an impulsive suicide is possible.

The environmental conditions under which this adolescent functioned should have been appraised for possible precipitating events. In this case, immediate contact with the school would have alerted teachers, counselors, and the administration to this student's vulnerability. Contact with the student's family might have brought to light the notes or other information that would have helped the intervenor assess the adolescent's risk more accurately.

In their desire to be thorough, some therapists prefer to go a step further when assessing adolescents who seem to be only moderately at risk. They inquire about what plan or method might seem most likely in the event of a more serious intent: "Well ... if you did seriously consider killing yourself, how would you do it?" Such questioning may elicit deeper signals as to the level of risk. When an adolescent can conjure a plan or method of self-destruction, suicide potential is generally greater. If the plan conjured from imagination is irreversible and lethal, it is prudent to increase estimations of risk level.

Interrupt the Suicide Process/Take Action

The specific action taken to interrupt the suicide process depends upon the level of suicide risk determined. Obviously, if the adolescent is in immediate danger, ensuring safety is the foremost goal. This may involve immediate networking with professionals for additional validation of assessment. It may involve not leaving the adolescent alone until the time for a professional consultation.

Interrupting the suicide process can be done by implementing three substeps: defusing negative emotions, opposing suicidal intent, and offering a plan for help.

Defuse negative emotions. The majority of suicidal individuals seem to be ambivalent about dying (Farberow & Litman, 1970; Suter, 1976). When the intervenor offers an empathic insight into the feelings of the suicidal adolescent, a defusion of the mass of negative feelings often occurs. Empathy tends to increase the overall persuasive potency of the intervenor. The following example illustrates this type of empathic insight:

Sandy, I think I can understand your feelings now—how all that confusion and fear has created a terrible pain in you ... so much that you're not certain anymore about whether you want to live or die.

Oppose suicidal intent. Once it has been determined that an adolescent desires, at some level, to die or escape pain through suicide, that intent must be countered and opposed firmly. This instruction may sound simplistic, yet at some time during the intervention process the helper must communicate opposition to the intended action. When the message that suicide is unacceptable is delivered empathically yet firmly, the suicidal adolescent often feels relief:

I'm so glad you've shared those feelings with me, Renee. You know I can't let you do anything to yourself—kill yourself. That's not an answer, but we can explore other options and help you put things back together.

Offer a plan for help. After defusing negative emotions and opposing suicidal intent, the next step is offering a concrete plan to help the adolescent. This involves sharing the intervention options with the youth. Having the adolescent choose between two or more treatment alternatives tends to restore some of the personal control temporarily lost during the suicide process. However, the intervenor may need to overrule the suicidal adolescent if he or she chooses an alternative that does not represent a valid life-saving strategy:

I can appreciate your wanting to keep this quiet and talk
only to your grandmother about it, but we need to remember that you were considering suicide and that's much too
serious to keep from your parents. We also need to get you
some professional help, and that will mean sharing your
pain with another person.

Although the adolescent might resist sharing his or her serious pre-
dicament with certain significant others, it must be kept in mind that
the suicide process often represents a closing of the adolescent's functional support system. Thus, a key ingredient in effective intervention
is helping the adolescent reopen and reaccess that system:

I know how difficult it will be to share this with your parents, but they have a right to know how bad you're feeling—
and even that you were considering suicide. I'll help you
tell them, Carlos. What do you think?

When the intervenor continues as primary therapist, assessment
findings must be reported to parents or guardians. If the primary intervention is taking place in the school setting—for example, through a
school counselor or social worker—the school administration must be
kept informed as well. It is also advisable to consult with another professional knowledgeable in suicide intervention and ethics prior to
starting treatment to validate the assessment findings, as well as on an
ongoing basis.

Obtain a Commitment

When both the adolescent and the intervenor agree on the nature
of the crisis as a life-threatening situation, it becomes necessary to solicit a reasonable level of compliance and commitment from the
adolescent:

Ben, you've been nodding your head throughout this, but I
need to hear from you how you feel about what I've pro-
posed. *(Pauses for response.)* I know this is a terribly difficult time for you, but we'll get you some help, and with
some time and hard work I think you'll be feeling much better.

If the adolescent is unwilling to comply with the recommended
plan, the intervenor should briefly review the perceptions of risk and
explain that there is no choice regarding interruption of the suicidal behavior. Additional negotiation may be necessary to determine mutually
agreeable steps that are within the framework of a bona fide treatment
program.

It may become necessary to negotiate an antisuicide agreement with the adolescent. An antisuicide agreement is a temporary restraining arrangement. Essentially, the intent of such an agreement is to extract a promise from the suicidal adolescent not to commit suicide and to make contact with the intervenor or another person if and when suicidal motivation resurfaces. This type of arrangement might appear transitory, but it can, and often does, help the adolescent by providing structure while other measures are implemented. It can give both the intervenor and the suicidal youth much-needed time.

What is agreed to, the time period, and any other content of the agreement must be clearly communicated to the adolescent (Hatton & Valente, 1984; Patros & Shamoo, 1989). Antisuicide agreements can be made verbally, or they can take the form of written contracts. An example of a verbal agreement follows:

> Melissa, I'm so glad that I've discovered just how unhappy you've been and what that unhappiness might have led to. Now that we're going to get you some help, I want you to promise me that you won't hurt yourself in any way or do anything that will endanger your life. Will you agree to that? *(Pauses for response.)* If you feel some of those same feelings and want to do anything to yourself, I want you to promise also that you will call me. *(Waits for answer and clarifies any confusion about agreement.)* Good, here is my phone number. Where can you keep it so that it's handy? I'll be at that number until tomorrow morning when I leave for school. You can reach me here then. If, for some reason, I'm not in my office and you need to get in touch with me, call _____ and he will know how to reach me. We can talk more about this agreement after you've seen Dr. _____ this afternoon and when we talk with your parents.

Figure 4.1 provides an example of a written antisuicide agreement. Many practitioners prefer the written contract because it adds a dimension to the agreement that a verbal contract does not have and requires a signature. It is important that everything in the contract be agreeable to both parties and that the contract be simple, easily readable, and provide for some means of validation or follow-up.

An antisuicide agreement also helps the intervenor assess the effectiveness of the intervention to that point. If an adolescent is unwilling to make such an agreement, it is then necessary to determine the reasons for resistance. The emergency precaution of hospitalization may be appropriate in such a case, as in the following example: During her appointment at a mental health center, a 19-year-old girl declared that

Figure 4.1   Sample Written Antisuicide Agreement

I promise not to hurt myself or attempt suicide.

I also promise to contact _____ at

_____ IMMEDIATELY upon feeling

depressed, hopeless, and in danger of harming myself in any way.

If _____ is not available,

I will contact _____ and discuss my

feelings and intentions.

This agreement is good for the time period

_____ through _____.

_____

(Signature)

_____

she would kill herself if her live-in boyfriend did not come back to her. Since the boyfriend was not available for an emergency appointment, the therapist attempted to extract an agreement from her not to harm or kill herself. The therapist enlisted the aid of another counselor and asked the client to repeat her story and her specific, irreversible suicide plan. After her consistent refusal to change her mind or to enter into a temporary antisuicide contract, the therapists informed her that she would have to be hospitalized. She was taken to the psychiatric unit, where she remained until her crisis passed and specific follow-up was arranged.

Make a Referral

The referral process demands that the intervenor have access to information about whom to refer and when. In the case of significant risk, an immediate referral to professionals who offer crisis services (clinics, hospitals, suicide prevention services, etc.) is necessary. When the risk is not as high, referrals are generally made to the same resources but with less urgency.

Follow Up

Many suicidal individuals who have received intensive therapy during the peak of their crisis take their lives after hospitalization or after initial intensive treatment. Follow-up is designed primarily to prepare the social support system for the individual's reentry and to use the information gained from the crisis to facilitate monitoring of the suicidal person. Effective follow-up, including systematic and intensive monitoring of the suicidal person, can help to save lives.

When making a referral, it is wise to arrange for both immediate and longer term feedback from the clinic or agency to which the adolescent is being referred. The parent or guardian must sign a release form that provides for information exchange. In an emergency situation, feedback is often spontaneous and accomplished without permission, but once an adolescent enters professional counseling and therapy, the rules of confidentiality prevail and a written release form is required. (The follow-up responsibilities of educators are detailed more specifically later in this chapter, under discussion of intervention steps in the school setting.)

Document and Report

The purposes of documenting the intervention experience are to facilitate the information flow to relevant parties and to protect the intervenor legally. Documentation of what happened during the assessment and intervention process is generally required when suicide intervention for an adolescent at any risk level is conducted by a professional (counselor, teacher, therapist) during the course of work-related activities.

Confidential information acquired during the course of a professional relationship can be shared with another person when there is serious reason to believe that the individual may harm himself or herself, or another person. Within the school setting the faculty member, pupil personnel specialist, or administrator who has become privy to the suicidal thinking of a student has both a strategic and ethical responsibility to consult with another person, thus breaking confidentiality. Professional organizations (i.e., the American Psychological Association, Association for Counseling and Development, National Association of School Psychologists, National Association of Social Workers) have documented ethical guidelines that reaffirm the client's right to privacy unless the criteria of endangerment are met.

Suicide intervention in the school environment includes reporting to and consulting with school supervisors and administrators. This facilitates productive planning and helps to protect the intervenor legally. Parents are contacted if, in the determination of the intervenor in consultation with the administration and other professionals, the student's level of risk is serious and if the school or state mental health policy provides for such an action. Parents or guardians of a minor maintain legal responsibility for their child and thus have the right to information that influences the child's health and, in some cases, the child's life (Brewer & Faitak, 1989). However, such a disclosure involves balancing the confidentiality of the professional relationship between the intervenor and the student and the legal right of the parent to have such information.

These general guidelines for intervention must be adapted to the specific situation. Unfortunately, the adolescent and intervenor may not have the time necessary to implement all of these suggestions. Following is a discussion of crisis intervention, applicable in situations in which general intervention strategies must be adapted to a much more urgent context.

CRISIS INTERVENTION STRATEGIES

The Nature of Crisis Intervention

The Chinese character for *crisis* represents two major concepts, danger and opportunity. By their very nature, suicidal feelings, thoughts, or actions represent danger for the adolescent. However, such a crisis also represents a potential turning point and thus an opportunity for growth and enrichment.

Both the manner in which a crisis is managed and the overall outcome have implications for immediate crisis reduction and long-term gain or loss. If the crisis resolution is maladaptive, the outcome generally will be negative, and vulnerability to future crises is increased. On the other hand, reaching an adaptive resolution tends to strengthen and enrich the adolescent's problem-solving abilities and emotional stamina.

Transcrisis Points

Typically, when an adolescent experiences a crisis, *transcrisis points* exist (Gilliland & James, 1988). These key turning points in the process of escalating to a higher level of crisis are minicrises that nonetheless require resolution. Suicidal behavior often results from the maladaptive resolution of a series of transcrisis points. Often, in retrospect, it is easy to see how the failure to resolve these transcrisis points adaptively should have indicated that the adolescent did not have normal coping mechanisms and was moving progressively toward suicidal ideation.

Transcrisis points may be difficult to assess because they do not necessarily proceed in a systematic and methodical fashion. An adolescent may, for instance, demonstrate a level of balance that suggests the crisis has passed when in truth there simply has been a respite period. If nothing productive occurred during the transcrisis point, the youth is left in an even more vulnerable emotional state. Each unsuccessful attempt to negotiate a crisis leaves the adolescent in a position in which the next stressor will undoubtedly be more difficult to resolve in a constructive fashion, progressively leading to suicide risk.

Consider the situation of an adolescent whose family moves just before his or her junior year in high school. The move results in relationship breaks with peers and school faculty. If the adolescent is unable to make connections at the new school, a sequence of transcrisis points including depression, poor grades, fights at school, substance abuse, and trouble with school faculty and law enforcement officials could result. At any of these points, the intervenor who notices the student's decline can interrupt the process and turn the youth toward recovery. If, however, the sequence continues uninterrupted as crisis after crisis passes unresolved, the student's feelings of hopelessness and worthlessness eventually may result in suicide.

Stages of a Crisis Episode

In order to intervene successfully, it is helpful to know the stages a crisis episode typically goes through. A psychological crisis often has a predictable pattern. Baldwin (1978) describes this pattern as the life cycle of a crisis. He suggests that there are four phases in any emotional crisis: (a) an emotionally hazardous situation, (b) the emotional crisis, (c) crisis resolution, and (d) postcrisis adaptation.

The following discussion examines each of these four stages and illustrates how one adolescent, Marilyn, might experience them. Marilyn is a 15-year-old high school freshman whose parents recently divorced.

Emotionally Hazardous Situation

When an individual experiences negative feelings (e.g., anger, helplessness, despair), the person experiences a simultaneous desire to reduce these feelings. The adolescent uses typical coping behaviors or thoughts in an attempt to reduce the unwanted feelings and to restore the balance of a precrisis state. If these coping attempts are ineffective, the next phase brings about an emotional crisis.

In Marilyn's case, her parents' divorce was the emotionally hazardous situation. In response, Marilyn felt discouraged and lost motivation to succeed in school.

The Emotional Crisis

When coping is inadequate, negative emotions persist and become exaggerated. The adolescent's thinking becomes confused and disorganized. In an attempt to resolve the crisis, new and different coping mechanisms may be sought. If these new coping attempts are unsuccessful, the crisis escalates.

Marilyn felt betrayed and rejected by her parents and began to seek approval and affection from Phil, a boy who had always been interested in her. The relationship quickly intensified as Marilyn sought his constant companionship and affection. Within weeks, they were physically intimate.

After several weeks, although still constantly in Phil's company, Marilyn began to feel tense and anxious. She was with him so much she had alienated her other friends through neglect. Despite the fact that initially she had sought Phil's companionship and thrived on his exclusive attention, she began feeling that there was something unhealthy about the relationship. As Phil grew more and more possessive and emotionally demanding, Marilyn's anxiety turned to panic.

Crisis Resolution

Maladaptive. Necessary support is either not found or not sought, and the coping mechanism used is not in the best interests of the adolescent. In such a case, isolation or withdrawal may occur, which temporarily assuages pain and hurt but eventually represents an unhealthy coping response. The support that might have been available remains unused. The adolescent is now at a more dangerous point than before.

Marilyn began to feel ashamed of and frightened by the implications of her new relationship. She felt cheap and trapped. As her anxiety intensified, she began to look for a way out of the trap. Shame and guilt kept Marilyn from consulting her friends, and since the divorce she felt unable to communicate with her parents, so she did not talk to anyone about her increasing helplessness and hopelessness.

Although Marilyn's mother sensed something was wrong and tried to reinstate a talking relationship, Marilyn's refusal to cooperate forced her to give up. She attributed Marilyn's moodiness to the trauma of the divorce and decided to give her some time on her own to work things out.

Marilyn's mood darkened, and she began to think that the only method of escaping her situation was suicide. Her self-destructive thoughts intensified her tension until she felt close to panic. She impulsively swallowed most of a bottle of a prescription cough syrup with codeine. She survived because her sister discovered her finishing the syrup and took quick action.

Adaptive. The adolescent is able to address the crisis and identify the source of the problem. Constructive coping mechanisms are identified, and the crisis is resolved. The adaptive resolution then reinforces productive coping skills, and new methods of adjustment are learned for use in future emotional crises.

In desperation, Marilyn turned to her mother, who knew that her daughter was in trouble. Marilyn's mother immediately made an appointment with the family doctor, who examined Marilyn and eliminated concern about pregnancy or disease. The mother, daughter, and doctor had a heart-to-heart talk defining many of the issues confronting the family, and the doctor recommended a family therapist. Marilyn opened new communication lines with both of her parents and was able to express much of her anger, resentment, and helplessness. With the support of her mother and professional therapeutic assistance, Marilyn was able to break off the destructive relationship and reinvest in constructive peer support.

Postcrisis Adaptation

Maladaptive. The adolescent does not attempt to resolve the crisis in an adaptive manner and is now burdened with that failure. The support required still does not exist, or the adolescent feels unable to seek it. If follow-up is not careful and comprehensive, the adolescent will simply return to the previously existing situation. This is particularly dangerous because, as noted earlier, adolescents leaving crisis care are more vulnerable to a repeated suicide attempt.

Marilyn revived to find herself the object of much unwelcome attention. Her mother was both guilt-ridden and angry at her, and her sister was hurt and confused. Her father came to see her and made the situation worse by heaping blame upon her mother. And, finally, Phil kept declaring his love and his determination to stick by her no matter what, becoming more possessive and suffocating than ever. As her personal relationships deteriorated further, Marilyn again began feeling that suicide was the best way out of her situation.

Adaptive. The adolescent has done what is necessary to cope with the problems precipitating the crisis and thus has become less vulnerable to future crises. New coping mechanisms have been incorporated, and the crisis evolves into a learning event.

Marilyn felt purged and cleansed after expressing her feelings in a supportive atmosphere. She now felt she could communicate much more effectively with her mother and was able to renegotiate her relationship with her father as well. She reported that, although it was a hard lesson, it was a real learning experience.

Marilyn's story illustrates how increased coping competency is achieved when the adolescent is able to resolve a crisis adaptively. However, as the example also shows, the opposite may also be true. Crisis proneness and vulnerability to suicide increase when an adolescent's coping efforts are maladaptive.

Steps in Crisis Intervention

Gilliland and James (1988) outline six basic steps in crisis intervention. These steps are presented here with specific applications to work with adolescents. There is significant overlap between crisis intervention and intervention in other circumstances; however, in crisis intervention accommodations are made due to the urgency of the situation.

Define the Problem

First, the intervenor must determine whether or not a risk of suicide exists and assess the risk level. This can be accomplished by making therapeutic contact and assessing for imminence, as detailed in the previous discussion of guidelines for intervention. Then the adolescent and intervenor must agree that there is a problem. For a therapeutic alliance to be formed, both must agree on the seriousness of the situation and a course of action.

For example, Lisa, a high school student, told her teacher about a conversation she had with her friend Tom at lunchtime. Tom had told Lisa that life was no longer worth living and he wished he was dead. The teacher kept Tom after class and disclosed the concern both she and Lisa had for him. She specifically inquired about Tom's thoughts and plans for suicide and discovered a very depressed, suicidal 15-year-old. The teacher told Tom that now that she knew how miserable he was, she couldn't just let him go without taking steps to get him some help. After some discussion, Tom agreed with her and the two began planning how they would tell his family and talking about the therapeutic options available to him.

Ensure Client Safety

Interrupting the suicide process is imperative. Such interruption may include defusing negative emotions, opposing suicidal intent, and offering a plan for help, as discussed earlier. But because this is a crisis situation, the intervenor should be prepared to implement a full range of emergency procedures, including first aid, if necessary. It is even possible that the intervenor will have to request that the adolescent surrender the means of suicide.

The following situation underlines the need to act decisively: A high school football coach was checking the locker room prior to turning out the lights and leaving. He discovered one of his senior players sitting alone in the corner of the locker room, half hidden by the open lockers. The coach sensed something was wrong when the athlete didn't respond to his joking inquiry about not wanting to leave the premises. After a brief conversation with the obviously morose youth, the coach noticed a bottle of pills in the student's hand. It was at that point that the coach realized the young man's intent and immediately requested that he turn over the pills. The coach drove the student home and stayed with the family until they all agreed to a meeting with the family physician on an emergency basis.

Provide Support

As in the general intervention strategy of making oneself psychologically and physically accessible, in a crisis situation the intervenor must serve the same function, becoming a critical human link who can communicate a basic message of genuine caring for the adolescent. Of course, this relationship must be formed more quickly than in a less urgent situation. For example, the intervenor might say, "Jamal, I've been very concerned about you lately. You seem so down and distant. I'd really like to talk with you and find a way of helping."

Examine Alternatives

When the adolescent is assessed as potentially suicidal, the intervenor must help him or her focus on a range of alternate approaches to suicide. If the adolescent can choose from an array of alternatives, it might help to reestablish some level of personal control. However, the intervenor needs to be ready to make choices for the adolescent if the student cannot or will not make a productive choice. For example, the intervenor might say, "Sally, it's really important now that we share this with someone else, someone who is trained to help you further with this. I'll go with you in either case, but would you prefer to talk with Ms. _____, the school counselor, or with Mr. _____, the school social worker?"

Make Plans

As in a less urgent situation, devising a therapeutic plan for the suicidal adolescent is the natural next step. This typically involves making a referral, initiating a suicide watch, and following the adolescent in a supportive role throughout and after the crisis period.

For example, one school psychologist assessed a 15-year-old student as being at moderate risk after she was referred for withdrawal, isolation, and possible depression. The student seemed relieved to be "discovered" and agreed to informing her parents and being referred on an emergency basis to the outpatient unit of the local hospital, which had an adolescent treatment unit. The school psychologist, along with the referring counselor, helped to coordinate and implement the intervention. The psychologist also organized a follow-up program that included outpatient counseling with the school's psychiatric social worker when the student returned.

Obtain Commitment and Follow Through

Effective and timely suicide intervention can all be for nothing if there is no commitment from the adolescent or concrete plan for which the adolescent is accountable. The commitment does not necessarily have to be a written antisuicide contract, as illustrated in Figure 4.1. However, some sort of a commitment must exist. A seriously suicidal adolescent will usually agree to being helped and is often greatly relieved to be connected to a support system.

In developing a treatment plan for a suicidal adolescent, whether in a crisis situation or not, care must be taken not to overburden him or her. If the adolescent is given too much responsibility for developing and implementing a problem-solving plan, he or she may experience increased pressure, retreat, and become suicidal again.

Once the intervenor solicits a firm commitment to a crisis plan from the adolescent, he or she needs to follow through in making sure that the adolescent, with help and support, is adhering to the plan. One middle school guidance counselor working with a depressed and frequently suicidal teenager requested that the student sign a contract, which they had written together, agreeing to call the social worker or a back-up counselor any time she began to feel "down, discouraged, despairing, or pity-prone." The social worker used the contract as part of the overall treatment to facilitate increased awareness of feelings associated with suicidal thoughts as well as to develop the student's commitment to counseling.

These crisis intervention steps can help the intervenor organize concrete and conceptually sound crisis intervention strategies. Note, however, that they do not address the need for evaluation of specific conditions of assessment that are the basis for successful suicide intervention. Gilliland and James (1988) suggest that the assessment process in this scheme is "overarching, continuous, and dynamically on-going throughout the crisis" (p. 23). According to this model of intervention, assessment is an essential component of the intervention process, and continual assessment is the primary tool used in proper intervention and referral.

INTERVENTION IN THE SCHOOL SETTING

Although most suicide attempts and completions occur away from school, the school can be an ideal arena in which to assess and intervene with suicidal adolescents. Nelson and Slaikeu (1984) suggest that schools are natural settings for crisis and suicide intervention because students spend as many waking hours with teachers and fellow students as they do with their families. In addition, the contact educators have with students is publicly sanctioned.

Changes in behavior may be recognized more clearly by peers and teachers than by family members (Allen, 1987). As noted in chapter 2, suicidal adolescents often have communication problems with their families that may propel them to communicate more of their distress to peers and/or educators. The importance of friends in the lives of teenagers was underscored by the results of the 1991 Gallup survey on teenage suicide. In this survey, a nationwide random and representative sample of adolescents were asked to rate the influence of nine factors (i.e., home, school, friends, music, religion, movies, magazines, books, and television) on their lives. Eighty-seven percent of the teen respondents reported that other teens are a major influence on their behavior. Only 51% reported that home exerted a great deal of influence, and 45% suggested that school was a major influence.

The criteria for intervention with suicidal youths in the educational arena are the same as they are for other settings—namely, the degree of lethality exhibited and the immediacy of risk.

Intervention During a Suicide Attempt

Whether or not the student has previously been identified as a suicide risk is not an issue when a suicide attempt is in progress. Life-saving strategies become the priority. Certain steps must be taken when a student has made a suicide attempt during school hours and within the physical and legal jurisdiction of the school. Discussion of the main steps in an emergency suicide intervention follows.

Step 1: Ensure the Attempter's Survival

The first priority should be to ensure the physical well-being of the attempter. This may include providing first aid, instituting life-saving procedures, and contacting emergency medical personnel (e.g., ambulance, emergency room, poison control hot line). A list of school personnel such as the school nurse or faculty with first aid and cardiopulmonary resuscitation skills should be available in all school buildings for such an emergency.

Step 2: Assess Method

Information on the method of the suicide attempt is critical for those initiating first aid. Paramedics and hospital personnel therefore should be apprised of the method used when the phone call is made. The answers to certain questions can be crucial in determining first aid: For example, in the case of a drug overdose, paramedics must know what drugs, how much, and when they were taken. For a self-inflicted stab wound, they must know the location and number of cuts and degree of bleeding. Providing as many such details as possible will increase the effectiveness of the first aid procedures used.

Step 3: Notify Parents or Legal Guardians

It is essential to notify parents or guardians as quickly as possible about their child's suicide attempt. Each school building should have a registration card with information on whom to contact and how. When parents or guardians are contacted, they should be told the nature of the emergency and the steps the school has taken.

Step 4: Activate the School Crisis Team

Every school should have a crisis plan to assist the faculty in dealing with frightened and concerned students, alarmed and inquisitive parents, and media inquiries, which are the inevitable result of a crisis (e.g., death of a student or teacher, school bus accident, etc.). An organizational plan for a school crisis team (SCT) is presented in chapter 5. The SCT coordinator should be informed immediately about the specifics of the crisis event. This notification should automatically initiate schoolwide, preplanned crisis activities.

Step 5: Document and Report the Crisis

The specifics of the suicide attempt, including details on the attempter, apparent method, procedures followed, and all individuals involved, need to be documented. To ensure continuity of care, school personnel need to provide information to any treatment agency or professional to which the adolescent is referred. This will likely require that parents or guardians sign a release of information form. A release of information form is legally advisable for the school system and required for primary care agencies such as mental health centers.

Step 6: Follow Up

Two basic levels of follow-up exist. In the first, school personnel need to be apprised of the immediate results of primary care in order to provide information to other students and parents. The designated SCT coordinator and/or school superintendent are the most logical school representatives to request such information from the emergency room, hospital, and family. As noted, release of such information usually involves the written approval of the family.

In the second level of follow-up, intermediate or long-term information is necessary from primary treatment personnel responsible for the student's therapeutic care. Such information is especially important when the student returns to school. The student will likely be sensitive to reentry, and faculty need to be advised about any unique issues or problems and the methods of addressing them. A staff meeting with involved outside agencies, teachers, pupil personnel specialists (e.g., counselor, nurse, school psychologist, school social worker), and administrators will help to prepare for this event and the student's anticipated ongoing needs.

For example, Nicole, age 13, had been referred to the junior high school guidance counselor for acting-out behavior—consistent belligerence, obstinacy, and refusal to follow rules. The school counselor had ascertained that Nicole's family life was in disarray. Her parents were involved in a complicated divorce involving allegations of domestic violence. Her brother had been arrested the previous week for auto theft.

The counselor scheduled an appointment for psychological testing and was in the process of consulting an adolescent mental health specialist who came weekly to the school to co-conduct group counseling with troubled students. Before they were able to arrange a meeting, Nicole attempted to kill herself. When discovered in the washroom, she had cut her arms severely above the elbow and was in the process of slashing her cheeks. She had written "help me" on the mirror with her own blood. The students who found her immediately ran to the principal's office. The school secretary called the local emergency number and the head of the SCT. The superintendent and school nurse were there within minutes to give first aid. The paramedics who arrived in response to the secretary's call assessed the wounds as superficial and transported Nicole, the SCT coordinator, and the principal to the hospital, where after being treated for her wounds Nicole was admitted to the adolescent psychiatric unit.

Later that day, the school psychologist, social worker, and counselor held a briefing session to provide teachers with information about the plan for explaining the circumstances surrounding Nicole's actions and her condition to the other students. Students were then told that Nicole had been distressed and had hurt herself in the lavatory but was in stable condition. Students were also told that if their parents needed information they could contact someone through a telephone number on a central bulletin board.

Assessment and Intervention With At-Risk Students

The preceding discussion offered information to be used in the case of a suicide attempt. Of course, intervention before an attempt is made is preferable. The following suggestions are for intervention with students suspected of being at risk. These seven assessment and intervention steps assist the intervenor in determining the level of suicide risk, as discussed at the beginning of the chapter, and in intervening in the suicide process.

Although a teacher or administrator initially may feel uncomfortable discussing suicide, by referring the student elsewhere too quickly the educator may suggest to the student that the problem is too great to deal with or too unpleasant to consider. To minimize feelings of discomfort, all school personnel should learn to conduct such interviews. If the interview is not handled properly, the student may have one more reason to avoid further help.

Step 1: Make and Maintain Constructive Contact

When an educator suspects that a student is imminently suicidal, he or she needs to initiate constructive contact with the adolescent. This contact must be made immediately, with tact, sensitivity, and firmness. Essentially, the intervenor communicates three important messages: "I hear what you're saying," "I take you seriously," and "I'm concerned about you." The intervenor should avoid alarming the adolescent yet must approach the situation seriously.

If there is time or opportunity, the educator should tell another faculty member, a student personnel specialist, or an administrator that a student is being assessed for suicide potential. However, in some situations it is not always possible or advisable for the teacher to talk to someone else until he or she has made an assessment of imminent danger. The assessment techniques for determining suicide risk discussed in chapter 3 need to be implemented here. The intervenor might begin by saying something like the following:

> I'm glad to get this opportunity to talk with you, Francis.
> I'm very concerned about you—the way you've been down
> and out of touch. After I read your essay, I became
> alarmed and wanted to talk with you. Tell me about what's

going on. Have you been thinking of doing anything to yourself, perhaps hurting yourself?

Constructive contact is also imperative with lower risk students because it serves as a bridge to communication. Such contact may help to defuse any level of suicidal thinking or distress related to previous thoughts about suicide. Conducting the suicide screening interview and establishing a relationship can also help to ensure effective referral and establish an ongoing relationship between the intervenor and the student.

Step 2: Assess for Imminence and Method

As previously noted, when the student has a definite suicide plan and method in mind, his or her potential lethality is considered very great. After making contact with the student, the intervenor should assess for the plan and method. The more concrete the plan and the more available the means, the greater the potential lethality. If the adolescent has the means of suicide immediately available, firmly ask the student to surrender it:

Carolyn, I'm so glad you've shared your feelings with me. It's important to me that we get you some help, but before we do that I want you to give me the pills from your purse. I can't let you walk around feeling this way with the means of taking your life.

With a lower risk student, the plans and method may be less well defined or even nonexistent. Therapeutic inquiries about how long the student has felt down, blue, or angry might assist in defusing the emotionality that has built up during the suicide process. Specific questions addressing the seriousness of intent need to be asked:

Tell me more, Jacob, about how long you've been feeling this way? *(Waits for response.)* Uh-huh—how serious were you about wanting to die (or hurting yourself)?

Even if the risk level appears to be very low, the student should be considered for counseling and ongoing therapeutic contact. If at any time the student develops more active suicidal thinking, the risk level can change very quickly.

Brian, I'm bothered by your mood today. You seem much more quiet, and I guess you seem to be down and discouraged. I need to know if you're having thoughts of suicide (or death, hurting yourself) again? *(Waits for response.)* How long have you been feeling that way?

Step 3: Consult With Another Professional

No single individual should assume all of the responsibility for intervening with a suicidal adolescent. A teacher should consult with a professional trained in suicide assessment and intervention as soon as possible. A consultation in which the symptoms are discussed can help clarify the level of risk, facilitate a more comprehensive plan of action, and allow for sharing of liability. The consultation process has two main benefits: The responsibility for assessment and intervention is shared, and the intervenor and professional provide each other with support and information during the arduous intervention process.

Step 4: Refer and Notify

When a student is determined to be or even suspected of being imminently suicidal, an immediate emergency referral should be made to a clinical specialist within the school system or to an appropriate specialist outside the system, such as the family doctor, mental health agency, or hospital outpatient clinic. Often a referral to the family doctor along with a personal phone call to the physician will make the alarmed adolescent and/or family more comfortable.

The family or responsible adult must also be notified immediately about the assessment and referral. It is particularly important to request that a family member or guardian personally take the student to the specialist and verify that this is done. Never allow a high-risk student to carry out the recommendation of seeing someone on his or her own.

When working with a student at moderate or low risk, consultation with a member of the pupil personnel services team or SCT clinician would be helpful. Most school systems employ counselors, school psychologists, and/or school social workers who have been trained in the assessment and treatment of depression and suicidal behavior (see Table 3.1). The guidelines for referral to one of these specialists include the mandate to notify the parents of such an adolescent.

A meeting with parents or guardians should be held as quickly as possible to inform them about the outcome of the assessment and to facilitate further psychological inquiry into possible causal issues. Ongoing contact with the parents or guardians may be necessary, especially if the school takes on the responsibility of primary treatment. In many cases a referral for family counseling is helpful. Even when family dynamics are not an issue, the family will be distressed and profoundly affected by the discovery of a suicidal member.

Step 5: Initiate and Organize a Suicide Watch

If a student is imminently suicidal, he or she should not be left alone. Once the student's psychological status has been determined, an intervention plan should be put into action. Under no circumstances should the student be sent for further assessment and treatment unaccompanied or be left alone to wait while things are arranged. Ideally, the individual who made initial contact with the student during the crisis should stay with the student until a family member or medical liaison person arrives.

Monitoring is a follow-up procedure that must start immediately after risk assessment. The student needs to be watched therapeutically from the time of discovery through referral and treatment. This may take a certain amount of networking among teachers, parents, and, in some cases, friends. Although it is necessary to monitor the suicidal adolescent, confidentiality is an important issue that cannot be ignored. The professional in charge of the case should be consulted about how far to go in involving the adolescent's peers and instructors in the suicide watch. Confidential information cannot be divulged without the prior written permission of the adolescent's parents or guardians. Even if permission is not required, as when informing the student's teachers, it is advisable to tell the student and his or her family what information will be shared and with whom.

The following sample inquiries illustrate how to facilitate peer, school faculty, or parent monitoring of the suicidal adolescent after a moderate or low suicide risk has been assessed.

Peers. "How has Jeff been doing, Alex? Does he seem to be OK with school/friends/activities?" *(Counselors, psychologists, and social workers may not divulge confidential information to students without prior written permission, but teachers can tactfully use this approach. Care must be taken not to violate the personal integrity of the suicidal adolescent and thus create more distress.)*

School faculty. "Now that we know how desperate Jeff has been feeling, Maria, we'll need to continue to monitor him. I'd like to check in with you each day *(possibly more frequently)* and see how he's responding in the classroom, to the other kids, and so on. He knows I'll be talking with you. I have his permission."

Parents/guardians. "Mrs. _____, I'd really appreciate it if we could talk frequently *(daily, weekly)* about how Jeff is doing at home. We do this any time we think any of our students get that discouraged. It helps us keep in touch with them and you."

Step 6: Record and Document

Everything pertaining to the events leading up to and including the disposition of referral must be carefully documented for the confidential student file. This is done to facilitate later information flow, which may be critical in the referral and treatment of the adolescent, as well as for the legal protection of the school district. The text of a sample confidential crisis follow-up note is as follows:

> Sandra _____ was released from the hospital Thursday, October 24, 1993. Mrs. _____ stopped by my office and told me that she thinks Sandra is feeling much better. She will not be attending school until Tuesday of next week. She is to be followed by Dr. _____. I have ascertained a release form will request a summary from Dr. _____ this day. I will request a staff meeting with her teacher, the school psychologist, building principal, and SCT coordinator for Monday afternoon. Mrs. _____ indicated that Sandra appreciated all of us sending cards and my visits to her during her hospital stay.

Step 7: Follow Up and Provide Aftercare Linkage

In follow-up and aftercare, it is important to continue to follow the student in an appropriate manner and assist in networking among everyone involved.

The importance of this step cannot be overemphasized. Too often the continuity of mental health care breaks down after the initial crisis intervention has been effectively implemented. Too often the monitoring of care is left to the family without the support of a therapeutic network. Ideally, there will be a liaison person in the school who has permission from the family to monitor aftercare and progress and to communicate with the primary therapist or counselor. Teachers and administrators need information about how to assist in the readjustment of the student during this very difficult time.

The parents or guardians need to be informed, and they have the right to any and all information. It is also important for the school to have the benefit of information regarding the outcome of the emergency referral and any plans for treatment that might follow. A tactful request to the parents regarding information about the outcome of the referral is important. The school liaison might say to a student's parent, for instance, "Mrs. _____, we're all very concerned about Charles. Would you please give me a call as soon as the doctor *(psychologist, psychiatrist)* determines what the next step is? We would also like to know how we can help."

The student may receive intensive therapy with a professional out-side the school and then be referred to one of the clinical specialists within the school system. When this occurs, a staff meeting with ap-propriate personnel should be arranged. The parents may also be in-vited to such a meeting to optimize the effectiveness of communica-tion. This linkage decreases the likelihood that a student will relapse without detection into the acute loneliness, hopelessness, and helpless-ness that led to the original suicidal state.

Liability Issues

School systems enjoy an unusual legal precedent with children. They are publicly mandated to provide institutional care during a major por-tion of a child's and adolescent's life. Parents literally turn their off-spring over to publicly employed professionals, who are then entrusted to provide educational and recreational activities. The physical and psychological safety of the child is presumed during these activities. When the physical and mental health of the student is jeopardized, cer-tain generally accepted procedures are implemented. When a student becomes physically ill during school hours, a referral to the office or school nurse occurs and a phone call is made to the parents or guardi-ans. Diagnosing the psychological state of the adolescent, however, is a more complicated task. Guidelines for determining what to do with a student when psychological impairment is suspected are not always clear. What is clear is that when a life is in jeopardy, the school system must provide every available resource to save that life. How that re-sponsibility translates into legal risk is the focus of the remainder of this chapter.

The basic concern must be the life of a student. As a society, we seem reasonably aware of the need to protect children and adoles-cents, but obviously suicidology is not an exact science. Administra-tors and educators need to know, as do all professionals, what their legal obligations are in the case of a suicidal student. The following points are generally accepted legal guidelines, but each state, and even certain school districts within states, may have different statutes or guidelines.

- School personnel are not responsible for the suicide death of a student unless they aided and abetted the student in death or during a period of obvious suicidality. This is interpreted as specifically assisting the student in at-tempting or completing the act of suicide by providing the means or by intentionally doing nothing, knowing that the suicide was going to occur.

- When a student is assessed as or suspected of being suicidal, the parents or guardians must be informed about the assessment and the actions being taken to alleviate or treat the vulnerability. This should be done as quickly as possible without jeopardizing the life of the student.

- When an employee or consultant to the school system becomes aware of the possibility of suicidal ideation in a student, he or she should consider immediate assessment and intervention. If this is not possible, immediate referral to an appropriate professional within or outside the school system should be made while the safety of the student is simultaneously ensured. The specific school administrator responsible for the student, such as the building principal, should always be apprised of suicide vulnerability and what staff and faculty are doing to counter the process with any student.

- The rules of confidentiality can be broken when information that suggests that a student is suicidal is obtained. The suspicion need only be slight, but it must be concrete. The statement or behavior that leads the educator to suspect a suicidal process needs to be documented. It is always prudent to err on the side of safety. Thus, breaking confidentiality to consult with a professional when suicidal ideation is suspected will result in a more effective assessment process.

- All communications, conversations, and actions taken with regard to the assessment, intervention, and referral of a suicidal (or suspected suicidal) student should be documented and recorded. These records should be kept in the student's confidential file. Some teachers and school clinicians keep what is known as "working files," which are not necessarily subject to legal seizure. However, if information regarding suicidal vulnerability remains only in a working file, the information does little to facilitate suicide prevention or intervention.

- When the suicide process is accurately assessed, regardless of risk level, the student should be referred to a therapist or clinic specializing in the evaluation and treatment of depression and suicide. Referral to professionals saves lives and provides educators with a measure of legal protection.

If all faculty, pupil personnel specialists, and administrators are trained in suicide assessment and referral, they might not be as hesitant to intervene with students for fear of legal troubles. Stated simply, educators are responsible for taking all signals and threats seriously and for acting professionally, effectively, and quickly on the information available. Following these guidelines should keep intervention in the school setting on firm legal footing. When all educators have access to the information and training they need in order to handle these types of situations, we will surely see a reduction in the loss of life.

SUMMARY

Interventions in the suicide process will depend in part on whether the adolescent is judged to be at low, moderate, or high risk. However, risk level is highly changeable, and any degree of risk must be viewed as serious.

Before implementing any intervention strategy, the intervenor must assess his or her beliefs and attitudes. Maintaining appropriate beliefs and attitudes is as important as possessing technical skills. When implementing general intervention strategies, following certain guidelines is advised. These guidelines concern being available, making therapeutic contact, assessing for imminence, interrupting the suicide process, obtaining a commitment, making a timely referral, providing systematic follow-up, and documenting and reporting the event and intervention.

In some cases, the adolescent is already in crisis. Crises result from maladaptive coping skills, which lead to depression and lack of self-confidence in the adolescent. Once an adolescent is in crisis, the same steps as for general suicide intervention must be taken, but with greater urgency. If an adolescent in crisis refuses to make a commitment to the intervenor, he or she may require hospitalization. It is also important to remember that large numbers of adolescents complete suicide after they have been hospitalized and released. Follow-up care and support are vital.

Detecting a suicidal adolescent is particularly likely in the school setting. Because students spend so much time in the school setting, educators should be trained in identifying signals of depression and suicidal ideation and in reporting and referring the adolescent. Schools should also set up a school crisis team, or SCT, in order to deal systematically with crises and disseminate information to other students, parents, and the media.

Educators must be prepared and professional in terms of assessment, intervention, referral, notification of parents and guardians, and follow-up. The legal responsibility of the school is to be vigilant in identifying a suicidal adolescent and in acting when one has been identified. Because negligence is a legal concern for school systems, error on the side of safety is recommended in terms of assessment, referral, and notification.

CHAPTER 5

The School Crisis Team

The previous chapter introduced the concept of the school crisis team (SCT) as an essential component of effective intervention in the school setting. This chapter will detail the mechanics of organizing the SCT and will discuss issues in SCT planning for suicide crises in the school. Because SCT planning must consider survivors' grief and mourning, the grief process is also examined. Specifically discussed are the basic components of prevention, intervention, and postvention as they relate to the function of the SCT. A case example of an SCT in operation completes the chapter.

THE SCT: BACKGROUND AND ORGANIZATION

The function and scope of responsibilities of an SCT typically include initiating school and community prevention programs, managing an ongoing crisis, and minimizing the trauma of a crisis or tragedy that affects the school's students, faculty, and staff. The SCT must become knowledgeable about and plan for almost any potential crisis or tragedy, and the development of such a team often involves many hours of research and organizational work. In brief, team organizers must develop expertise regarding the components of emergencies and crises and the requirement of planning the most effective prevention, intervention, and postvention strategies.

Historical Development

When an alarming increase in adolescent suicide came to the attention of the public in the 1980s, a number of legislative efforts established, in piecemeal fashion, the groundwork for more massive prevention and intervention efforts by the federal government. The four-volume *Report of the Secretary's Task Force on Youth Suicide* provided comprehensive recommendations for the professional and lay community to reduce the rate of adolescent suicide. According to Frazier (1989), the task force yielded the following recommendations:

1. To increase data development related to adolescent suicide

2. To expand research into the area of risk factors

3. To evaluate the effectiveness of current intervention measures

4. To facilitate support in the area of intervention services

5. To develop measures for public information and support

6. To increase the involvement of both public and private sectors in the prevention of youth suicide

The task force acknowledged the difficulties of implementing such measures without funding and defined the complexities inherent in the overall problems of prevention. Nevertheless, several states, such as California and Illinois, immediately began requiring suicide training for educators and administrators. Out of such training evolved the concept underlying SCTs—crisis management teams within the school.

Purpose and Intent

The purpose of the SCT is to manage and control any crisis event that affects members of the school system. A crisis can be any trauma that occurs during school time and on school property, and that directly or indirectly affects students, staff, faculty, or administration. Such crises include, among others, suicide attempts or completions, hostage taking, or homicides. Such events pose both physical and psychological dangers requiring immediate, intelligent responses that can result only from prior planning.

Other crises may initially occur away from the school setting but may also mandate school-related assistance. Examples of such events include the death of a teacher, a school bus accident, or a serious automobile accident involving students or school personnel. The SCT's comprehensive crisis plan enables the school system to provide quickly and efficiently for both the physical and psychological needs of the students, staff, and faculty. Such preparedness on the part of the school will prevent the crisis from escalating and will minimize shock in the aftermath of crisis. Without such a mechanism in place, rumor and uncertainty can lead to panic. Consider, for example, the observation of a high school principal after a car accident involving four students:

> When the four students were killed, there were so many rumors throughout the community that we had a great deal of trouble just getting the story straight. For example, some

kids had heard that the entire basketball team had been killed! It was a mess and created an atmosphere of hysteria before the kids and teachers found out what really happened. I believe that the panic and misinformation about the incident made everyone's adjustment more difficult even after the rumors were put to an end.

Crisis Team Personnel

The first step in creating an SCT is selecting the personnel who will be involved. A comprehensive crisis team must include representatives from all components of the educational unit, as well as community organizations and agencies (Garfinkel, 1989). The SCT is designed to provide the broadest coverage possible within the school system for information dissemination and crisis management. Typically, the following school system personnel should be represented:

- The school administrative office, including the superintendent and/or delegated assistants
- The building principals and/or vice principals
- Faculty representing all buildings and grade levels
- Support staff (e.g., secretarial, food service, janitorial, transportation)
- Pupil personnel staff (e.g., school psychologists, social workers, counselors, and nurses)

Community members that should be represented include the following:

- Emergency personnel (e.g., police, firefighters, hospital staff, ambulance drivers)
- Physicians and psychologists, to act as consultants and emergency resources
- Social workers, human services workers, and counselors, to broaden the pool of consultants
- City or township administrators, to provide liaison with the larger community
- The media, who must be made aware of how their coverage of the crisis could affect vulnerable adolescents
- PTA or PTO representatives

Before the actual planning stage can begin, it is important that SCT members have some general knowledge of the grief and mourning process. This knowledge is as essential in informing SCT development as is knowledge of crisis management. Therefore, before the prevention, intervention, and postvention functions of the SCT are detailed, discussion will focus first on the grief and mourning process.

THE GRIEF AND MOURNING PROCESS

Grief and mourning are the inevitable result of a suicide attempt or completion. The loss of a daughter, son, student, or friend precipitates a period of grief and mourning that may be predictable but is nevertheless extremely painful and problematic (Rando, 1984). The suicide of a young person meets the criteria for the type of death that severely complicates survivors' mourning and adjustment. There are several reasons for this:

- The suicide is generally unexpected.

- The death of a young person is harder to accept than that of an older person who has lived a full life.

- Suicide is incomprehensible and perhaps even morally wrong to many, especially when involving a youth.

- The suicide completor's family and friends are left with guilt, anger, and a sense of unfinished business with the deceased, which they must work through.

- There is less social support for a suicide completor's family than there may be for other bereaved families because of blame unjustly assigned the family.

Thus, suicide by a young person is very difficult for survivors. In addition to the "wrongness" of a child's predeceasing a parent, suicide often reflects perceived failures: the failure of the deceased to cope adequately with life, the failure of others to detect a problem and successfully intervene, the failure of family, friends, or the school system to provide a nurturing and meaningful environment. This situation is exacerbated by traditional social stigmas regarding suicide (suicide is immoral, the family should be ashamed, etc.). These stigmas further inhibit the survivors' healing process. The result of complicated mourning is that survivors must work harder to reconcile to the death, to feel that they can let go of the deceased, and to move forward in their own lives.

When a suicide occurs in a school setting, the grief reaction is often further complicated by the group response of fellow students and school personnel or by the institutional response of the school and administration. In order to be more sensitive to these issues in designing prevention, intervention, and postvention procedures, educators and parents should be aware of the stages of grief and mourning (Rando, 1984; Schneider, 1984). It is important to note that not all survivors will exhibit all of these stages in exactly this order; however, the following stages are generally observed in some form.

Denial

Denial is a common reaction to any death. Variations on the statement "No, it just can't be true" are common psychological responses that help the individual absorb traumatizing information. Eventually, reality prevails, and the survivors are forced to face the fact that a loved one is dead.

Although acceptance of unexpected death is always difficult, the acceptance of a suicide is particularly problematic. A survivor may eventually accept the fact of death but continue to deny the reality of self-inflicted death. Thus, denial may continue in a fragmented way. Survivors may indulge in magical thinking, feeling that the deceased will return or appear unscathed. Symptoms of denial may manifest themselves through avoidance of the funeral or discussion of the trauma.

Denial generally diminishes with time, particularly in the presence of others who accept the death. Gentle and constant support will provide an atmosphere where a denial-oriented survivor can more easily come to his or her own level of adjustment about the suicide. It is important to understand and empathize with any survivor and not force the reality of the death on a defended person. Facilitating some level of positive discussion about the deceased might help the survivor begin to come to grips with the suicide.

Eventually, the survivor may merely accept the death but not the suicide. As long as this survivor is not hampered by this belief in moving forward in his or her life, limited acceptance is not necessarily damaging. However, if denial does not incorporate any elements of reality and/or continues for an extended time, professional intervention may be warranted.

Anger

Suicide frequently produces anger in survivors, which may be pointed in many directions. "If he hadn't been drinking at that bar," "It's her fault for breaking up with him," and "The school should have known" are just some of the expressions of rage that help survivors externalize their turmoil. Like denial, anger is a defense against pain and must be anticipated to some degree. When that anger turns inward, it may also manifest itself in lethargy, inertia, and depression.

Allowing and facilitating expression of anger at themselves, others, or even the deceased should be encouraged in survivors within an appropriate context. Parents, relatives, and friends have the right to feel anger at the injustice of the death. When anger begins to be expressed, it may reflect progress in the healing process and therefore needs to be addressed in a nondefensive and reflective way. Knowledge of another's anger about the suicide also reassures survivors that they have a right to such feelings and that expressing them is appropriate. Eventually, however, for healthy adaptation to take place, survivors' fury and rage need to be directed toward the act of suicide itself and not at themselves, others, or the deceased.

Depression

Depression is a natural response to any major loss. Depression may occur immediately or several weeks after the death and may last for days, weeks, or even months depending on the closeness of the relationship (e.g., relative, friend, acquaintance) and the status of the relationship at the time of the suicide (e.g., healthy, marginal, conflicted). If the relationship between the survivor and the deceased was conflicted at the time of death, there is a much higher probability that the survivor will become depressed and remain depressed until any unfinished business with the deceased can be worked out.

Although the feelings of sadness, hopelessness, and helplessness that generally result from losing an important person are normal, there is a point at which a depressed survivor may require treatment. If depression becomes severe (i.e., the individual is not adapting to the loss or is harmful to self or others) or chronic (i.e., the individual is depressed for 6 months or more), the survivor should be referred to a physician or therapist. It must be noted that lack of depression in a survivor can also indicate a complication in mourning. This may signal an adaptive response but may also indicate a defensive posture or denial. Other bereaved individuals or survivors may misread this response as indifference or coldness and further complicate the survivor's adjustment.

Facilitating return to a normal schedule and encouraging the survivor to participate in some activities is recommended. Mourners should be encouraged to avoid the tendency to survive without help or support. Unfortunately, the social support that many bereaved individuals receive is not there for survivors of suicide, who are too often avoided or blamed. Whatever social support there is should be taken advantage of. In addition, the bereaved can be put in contact with nearby support groups for survivors of suicide. These groups can provide both contact and comfort.

Survivors are victims, too, subject to anger at the deceased, guilt, and denial of the suicide. These complicating variables make them vulnerable to depression and maladaptive coping techniques to lessen their pain. In my work with grieving survivors I find it helpful to encourage positive thoughts about the deceased. Working through depression involves both self-forgiveness and forgiveness of the deceased. Certain reflections about the positive aspects of the relationship might help to break through negative obsessions about the loss. Of course, if extreme depression continues for a long period of time, referral to a qualified professional is advisable.

Acceptance

Acceptance—sometimes called *resolution*—is a phase of mourning that indicates a more complete awareness of the extent of the loss and an ability to function adaptively without the deceased. This stage is marked by a willingness to discuss the loss more openly and with less obvious pain and discomfort. At this point, friends and classmates may elect to invest themselves in suicide prevention programs such as peer counseling, or they may use their positive energy to create a memorial to the deceased student. Mourners who integrate a healthy acceptance of the loss have generally redefined their relationship with the deceased. That redefinition incorporates a willingness to move forward with their own lives without guilt or burden.

The mourning process can be long, complex, and painful. Although denial, anger, and depression are all normal responses to the death of a loved one, educators must learn to use their best judgment with this vulnerable population. Students who continue to obsess about the deceased or who display acute depressive symptoms should receive immediate therapeutic attention. Because cluster suicides are not uncommon (see chapter 1), it is particularly important that educators intervene when a student's mourning appears complicated.

Actual planning of the SCT's prevention, intervention, and postvention activities can begin once the SCT is adequately educated in the grief and mourning process and is able to integrate that knowledge into its activities.

SCT PLANNING FOR SUICIDE CRISES

A school's comprehensive suicide crisis plan will involve three basic levels of crisis involvement—prevention, intervention, and postvention.

The specific tasks in each area will vary depending upon such factors as the size of the student body, resources required for specialized training, and available community resources and support. The following guidelines relate specifically to crises involving suicide attempts or completions.

Developing the Plan and Program

Once the SCT members are assembled, designing a schoolwide suicide prevention, intervention, and postvention program must begin with the writing of a program philosophy and the development of a support base. The SCT's practices must be preceded by a well-organized statement that addresses the following issues:

- The overall problem of youth suicide in the United States
- The relevance of such a problem to the specific school district
- The general and specific reasons a program needs to be implemented
- The goals of the program and the methods of goal attainment
- The means by which program methods and outcomes can be evaluated

The team needs to define types of crises, develop plans for each major type of crisis, and establish both a generic flow chart and a flow chart specifying responsibilities for each type of crisis. Many such plans have been developed in schools in response to student suicides (e.g., Klingman & Eli, 1981; Kneisel & Richards, 1988; Lamb & Dunne-Maxim, 1987; Ojanlatva, Hammer, & Mohr, 1987).

Areas of crisis response must also be determined. Several important areas of response include emergency procedure liaison (with both trained personnel in the school and professionals outside of it); containment of the crisis, in terms of both geography and information dissemination; notification of family members; student care; and postvention, in terms of providing therapeutic opportunities for crisis survivors to discuss and work through the crisis.

With these areas of crisis response identified, members can begin to assign responsibilities. Kirk and Shatz (1990) list the following specific responsibilities of key SCT members or coordinators.

Administration. The district administration maintains overall responsibility for crisis management and usually delegates specific crisis responsibilities to various units and personnel within the system.

Crisis team coordinators. SCT coordinators typically include a member of the school superintendent's office and one representative, usually the principal or an assistant principal, from each building in a school district. The function of the building coordinator is to oversee crisis management within his or her assigned facility and to receive and disseminate information from various building and community units. A backup coordinator should be assigned to provide leadership when the building coordinator is not available or is engaged in direct crisis intervention.

Faculty and staff. Responsibilities are assigned depending upon areas of expertise and contact with students and community. Counselors and psychologists might be used in direct intervention or support of faculty, who would be assigned direct care of students. School social workers might be assigned duties associated with community liaison or family support. The school nurse would be the likely candidate to coordinate medical intervention and provide liaison with paramedics. Principals and unit administrators are often important conduits for information dissemination with the media and community.

Communication among all parties during a crisis is necessary, but information should be channeled through the administration and/or coordinators. For example, if a parent asks a question of a faculty member during or after a crisis, that question would be directed to the building coordinator, who would in turn maintain constant contact with the coordinator at the superintendent's office.

Following are some specific organizational suggestions for the SCT:

- Design a team approach that provides for prevention, intervention, and postvention.

- Designate the SCT coordinators in advance.

- Involve a diverse core of experienced individuals in the crisis team.

- Maintain a resource list, available to all school personnel, with names, addresses, and phone numbers of critical referral resources. A flow chart of priority contacts should be included in the list.

- Designate a central meeting place for the SCT. This place should have multiple phone lines.

- Meet regularly to review and update procedures and to conduct occasional practice alerts involving different kinds of crises.

- Provide for an all-school inservice crisis management training session, with an emphasis on prevention as well as intervention and postvention.

- Assign crisis tasks to appropriate team members. These tasks should include the duty of recording the event as specifically as possible.

- Provide advanced training for SCT members assigned tasks that demand such training. For example, offer training in the following areas: (a) legal issues related to certain kinds of crises; (b) communicating sensitive information to family members (i.e., a child's suicide attempt); and (c) staff guidelines during initial stages of all types of crises.

Prevention Tasks

Prevention tasks for the SCT include designing and implementing suicide prevention programs and providing training for students, faculty, administration, support and clerical staff, and parents. Such activities generally include identification of students at risk, assessment for risk level, intervention, and referral procedures.

Additional prevention tasks include the following:

- Soliciting support of parent groups and providing education and training for parents and family members

- Arranging a community education program in cooperation with community resources such as mental health clinics or hospitals

- Establishing liaison with appropriate community resources (mental health professionals, the media, etc.)

- Creating student assistance programs and conducting peer counseling training for students

- Developing ongoing information updates and skill maintenance programs, and performing periodic program evaluations

- Acquiring and updating a comprehensive set of reference materials (books, journal articles, reprints, audio and video training materials) on adolescent suicide that can be made available to faculty and students

- Providing interested community members and agencies (media, police, mental health professionals) access to these reference materials for research, presentations, and program development

Intervention Tasks

Intervention training is not unlike prevention; both areas emphasize assessment and referral. With intervention, however, the emphasis is on therapeutic relationship building, and the training in suicide intervention methods is more focused.

Some objectives of intervention are as follows:

- Providing support and funding for pupil personnel specialists who can facilitate intervention skill enhancement

- Providing training for faculty, staff, and students (peer counseling) in assessment and intervention procedures

- Developing a prototypical profile of the high-risk student to assist teachers and students in identifying such students

- Acquiring the assistance of appropriate professionals in the community (therapists and suicide specialists) to serve when needed as on-site or off-site consultants

- Maintaining liaison with community resource and support agencies and groups

- Training faculty, staff, and peer counselors in assessment interview techniques and what to do for students with varying levels of risk

- Developing a comprehensive model of crisis management for the SCT and implementing it when necessary

Postvention Tasks

The typical questions of the school and community after an adolescent suicide are "Why did this happen?" "How can we prevent a recurrence?" and "How can we provide the most support to survivors?" The intent of postvention is to counteract a repetition of the event(s) that precipitated the crisis and to provide the maximum help to survivors. Thus, postvention is concerned with programmatic efforts to assist and support survivors of suicide.

Survivor Support Groups

Once a suicide has been attempted or completed, one effective way of facilitating discussion and observing how students are progressing in their mourning is by organizing a survivor support group. Such groups, often organized and sponsored by human service agencies or hospitals, can offer potentially powerful healing experiences. One of the many advantages of such groups is that survivors can express feelings that are typically similar to those of other survivors. The therapeutic benefit of such sharing is increased empathy among survivors and the opportunity to offer mutual assistance and support. In addition, through such groups, educators can monitor students' progress in mourning and identify those students who may need extra help in working through the loss. In some cases it may be advantageous to offer such a group for faculty as well. For a rationale and guidelines for developing support groups for students and school personnel, see Kirk and Walter (1981).

Memorial Services

Sometimes it is appropriate for the school to be involved in planning a memorial service. This is often done as a form of postvention therapy, allowing students, faculty, and staff a chance to have input in designing the service and to say good-bye to the deceased in a familiar context. Planning for a memorial service should sensitively integrate the wishes of the family with the expressed needs of students. The arrangements related to memorial services at the school should also be made with certain clinical concerns in mind. For example, the over-dramatization of a death may negatively influence student acceptance and adjustment and possibly even serve to accelerate an already existing suicide process in other students.

A designated SCT member may be an appropriate liaison with the family during the planning of such a service. If the family has a working relationship with a teacher or administrator not on the SCT, it might behoove planners to have that person coordinate family wishes and student plans.

The following specific questions need to be addressed in planning memorial services:

Where should the service be held? Some school systems, in their collective grief, prefer to have a vigil in a school building. In some cases, this has included viewing the body. This practice is not recommended as it may bewilder already grief-stricken students and exacerbate grief issues. On the other hand, the healthy grief process may be enhanced by a sensitive and appropriate memorial service held on school grounds.

Who should attend the service? A determination of who should attend the memorial service should emerge from mutual consultation with the administration, faculty, and certain students (i.e., friends or student senate, team, or activity members). It is advisable, however, for the SCT to make recommendations to grieving friends and family.

When should the service take place? Such services are often held within a week of the funeral. Waiting much beyond that time risks continuation of the immediate grief response and thus could be antitherapeutic.

If done sensitively and with the needs and desires of the students in mind, a memorial service can have therapeutic benefits unobtainable through other postvention practices. The formality, function, communal nature, and locality of such a service often help relieve some of the burden of grief and guilt and provide a sense of closure.

Ongoing Follow-Up

The death of a student, particularly a suicide, is a traumatic and overwhelming event for many students and faculty. It is important to maintain perspective both during and after the trauma. The following suggestions should be considered in this context.

When the immediate crisis has passed, the SCT must address the longer range tasks of (a) assisting in the psychological autopsy (in cooperation with the coroner's office), (b) helping to coordinate a systemwide suicide watch for high-risk students, and (c) continuing to address the needs of a grieving student body. It is important to individualize follow-up strategies for each suicide crisis. The SCT, in consultation with the school administration, may wish to consider some of the following options:

Developing processing or ventilating opportunities for certain students and/or faculty. In some instances affected survivors may opt for individual therapeutic support away from the school setting, but school counselors may wish to offer such a service to invited students or hold open-ended discussions on a regular basis for individuals who wish to attend. The potential benefit of such experiences is that grieving persons may not only receive support from others but may also experience the therapeutic advantage of offering solace to others who have similar psychic pain.

Sponsoring school-supported open forums. An open forum can include students who wish to discuss grief issues or topics related to depression and suicide in a public arena. Panel discussions that involve experts in the areas of crisis, adolescent stress, substance abuse, and other related topics can facilitate worthwhile discussions among concerned students, family members, and faculty.

Conducting discussion in certain school classes. Classes in family relations, health, psychology, sociology, and the like may be ideal places to encourage discussions about suicide, death, grief, and mourning rituals.

Arranging for cooperative community/school ventures. Such cooperative ventures could include, for example, ongoing courses or discussions, or a public health series focusing on the broad issue of teens at risk or more specific issues in suicide prevention. A series of articles written for the local newspaper could also help to open the issues to a broader arena.

As always, the message to be communicated during follow-up activities is that suicide is unacceptable. It must continually be stressed that suicide is the worst possible choice available among the array of options for young people. We can best encourage adolescents to explore other options by continuing to stress this point and by providing accessible alternatives.

OVERVIEW OF SCT INTERVENTION PROCEDURES

The following procedural descriptions indicate the way an SCT should respond to a suicide attempt and a suicide completion. There is, of course, a certain amount of overlap in the procedures in each of these instances.

Suicide Attempts

The first step that should be taken after a suicide attempt is verification of the attempt. The level of lethality of the method should also be determined, as well as the adolescent's commitment to death. This information is very helpful in obtaining proper medical assistance, making an appropriate referral, and conducting follow-up.

While the attempter is receiving medical and/or psychological assistance, parents or guardians should be notified. They should be told the specifics of the attempt and what response procedures are being followed. In some cases, the student may be en route to the hospital and parents will have to go there, whereas in less serious cases parents may be called to the school to meet with their child, a member of the pupil personnel team, and possibly an administrator.

Maintaining the student's right to confidentiality potentially complicates the next step, informing students and staff about the attempt. However, all appropriate faculty and staff should be informed. The decision to tell the student body about the attempt may rest upon how public the attempt was and the degree to which the other students were affected. If students know of the attempt, friends and/or siblings of the attempter should be spoken to individually and perhaps released for the day. Other students can more appropriately be given information and support in the classroom setting. Ongoing monitoring of any designated high-risk students is important.

The SCT member designated as liaison between the referral source (mental health professional, therapist, hospital) and the school will need to follow the student's progress for as long as necessary or possible. To do so, he or she will need to obtain signed release of information forms from the student's parents or guardians.

Finally, preparation for the student's reentry is essential, with the SCT providing the organizational structure. Teachers (and certain selected students) may need to be given specific instructions and recommendations by the therapist or treatment team. This information is best shared in the form of a comprehensive staffing involving the returning student's teachers, pupil personnel specialists, and a representative of the treatment team (preferably the student's therapist). Planning should focus on what will need to be done for the student to reenter the school environment with the least fuss and most support possible.

There should be a plan for monitoring the student on his or her return to school. This is best accomplished through a team approach (teachers, principal, counselor, parents, selected friends) coordinated by a member of the pupil personnel unit. Again, the student's right to privacy must be respected. Although pertinent information can be revealed to trustworthy individuals who play an integral role in the student's recovery, indiscriminately revealing the details of the attempter's personal pain and randomly enlisting the aid of students and faculty is inappropriate and potentially damaging to the attempter. Such practices may also be illegal.

Suicide Completions

The overall effect of a student's suicide on fellow students, faculty, and staff depends on several factors: how, when, and where the student died; the class the student was in; and the social status of the completor. When a student completes a suicide on school property, during school hours, and/or with witnesses, the complications are increased. The more physically damaging the method was, the more difficulty survivors and witnesses have in adjusting. If the student was in a higher class, perhaps a senior, and thus was fairly well known by both students and faculty, mourning may be more difficult for survivors. And, finally, the more popular and influential the suicide completor was in the school setting, the more survivors will feel his or her loss. In all cases, survivors are victims and need therapeutic assistance and aftercare.

The procedures after a suicide completion involve both short-term and long-term tasks. If the suicide takes place on school grounds, a priority must be contacting emergency medical personnel (paramedics, hospital, police, and/or the coroner's office). The death should be verified as a suicide and the parents or guardians notified as soon as possible. A designated SCT member may be asked to accompany the coroner or police for notification of parents or guardians. The SCT as a group should also be assembled for an emergency session to implement suicide postvention procedures.

The school's faculty and staff should be informed about the suicide completion through the prearranged information dissemination network. Teachers who will inform the student body of the completion must be identified. Friends and siblings of the student should be told privately by a member of the SCT or a designated teacher.

The community response team and PTA/PTO organization should also be notified to stand by. The specific role of previously designated PTA/PTO members should remain flexible—essentially, as needed, these individuals serve as familiar liaisons with other parents and the community.

It is advisable to quickly dispel rumors that will likely emerge throughout the building, school system, and community. Here the SCT is vital in providing specific but appropriate information. Students should get a statement within a reasonable time (e.g., immediately if the suicide occurred in the building, the last class period in other buildings, the next day if the suicide occurred overnight). Students who are considered most affected by the suicide (friends, siblings, students identified as being themselves at risk for suicide) should be given immediate therapeutic attention, with provisions for long-term care also being made available.

A systemwide faculty meeting should take place as soon as possible to plan strategy and disseminate information. Community consultants can provide assistance in such a meeting. If support staff cannot attend the faculty meeting, separate meetings may need to be organized quickly to provide information and recommend methods of answering questions and responding to statements about the death. Support staff are in an ideal position to assess students' reactions to the death and to evaluate morale. They should not be overlooked as valuable participants in the SCT's operations.

Arrangements must also be made for follow-up and monitoring within the school system and the community. Here the important task is coordination among institutional and community resource personnel to prevent or intervene in possible cluster suicides. Community human service agencies will very likely intensify their suicide watch with high-risk individuals. This should be done in the school setting as well.

The general content of press releases should be prearranged (i.e., before a specific occurrence) with local media. The main consideration here is not to overdramatize a student's death. This caution is based on the finding that the manner in which a suicide is made public may negatively influence an already suicide-prone individual (Davidson & Gould, 1989). Media representatives need to be apprised of this danger during the preplanning stage so that they will be sensitive to these issues when and if the situation actually arises.

In the following hypothetical case example, having the SCT available allowed a school district to minimize the escalating confusion and crisis atmosphere that otherwise would have occurred. Such a trauma mandates that a maximum effort be made to maintain psychological and logistical balance. Having developed specific steps to deal with such a crisis helped maximize the resources and support services available and cut down on the time each step took to accomplish.

CASE EXAMPLE: THE SCT IN ACTION

Randy, age 17, seemed relatively well adjusted until his sophomore year of high school. The previous summer he had been a volunteer working with disadvantaged minority children in a large metropolitan area. Upon his return, his teachers and friends noticed a change in him. His circle of friends slowly shifted from college-bound peers to a drug-oriented group. He became sullen, rebellious, and uninterested in school. Referrals to school counselors brought only opposition, and meetings with Randy's mother did not seem to change things. He was arrested once for possession of marijuana and carrying a concealed weapon—a switchblade—to school.

After this incident, Randy was sent to a school psychologist for evaluation. The psychologist determined that Randy had a behavior disorder and referred him for treatment at a local human services agency. Randy attended only two meetings for troubled adolescents before he refused to return. His mother's efforts remained ineffectual. After their repeated attempts to intervene met with failure, teachers and administrators became indifferent. They settled for a short-term disciplinary measure with Randy—suspension.

During his junior year, Randy had a particularly vicious argument with a former girlfriend in the school cafeteria. After the argument, he left school, only to return with a .22 caliber pistol. He walked into the class his former girlfriend was in and threatened the entire class with the gun.

A student who had seen Randy enter the classroom with the gun ran and told the principal about it. The principal sent the assistant principal to verify the student's observation. The assistant principal, knowing only that there was an armed student in the class, entered the room. Randy panicked and shot the assistant principal in the leg and then turned the gun on himself, shooting himself in the head. The classroom teacher quickly sent another student to the principal's office to relay these events.

The designated SCT building coordinator was the principal. She followed the procedure the SCT had laid out by first attempting to verify the crisis. Once she had verified the incident, she put the SCT plan into action.

Each building within the school district had included secretarial staff in the crisis management training, and each of these staff members had been assigned responsibilities in the event of a crisis. The principal's secretary called the police and paramedics, who also had been involved in the crisis management planning. The two other building secretaries were put on alert. One placed an immediate call to the administration building, where the SCT administrative coordinator (the assistant superintendent of schools) set into motion certain prearranged crisis steps: All phone lines were cleared with the exception of the phone line to the crisis-origin building; another phone call was placed to the police and paramedics en route to provide them with a status report and more details of the crisis than could be given in the first phone call.

Meanwhile, the principal in the crisis-origin building announced over the public address system a prearranged code for an ongoing crisis in the building. This alert resulted in each teacher's closing off or returning with students to his or her classroom. SCT members who were not engaged in teaching or directly responsible for students went to the principal's office immediately to consult and make themselves available to assist if needed. After ensuring that the crisis management plan was on track, the principal left for the classroom where the incident had taken place.

The classroom teacher at the scene was in the process of systematically removing students from the room to ensure safety and restore order. The school nurse, who had been admitted to administer first aid, discovered that the assistant principal's wound was superficial but that Randy's wound had been fatal. The principal returned to her office to direct the crisis response.

Once back in her office, the principal used the open phone line to the administrative office to verify the crisis and update the administrative SCT coordinator. Upon receiving this information, the administrative SCT coordinator set into motion preparation of the crisis-team room and made calls to the systemwide SCT members with all available information.

The administrative SCT coordinator also called the school transportation unit, and available personnel (assistant director, secretary, chief mechanic) were immediately dispatched with school buses to the school for a stand-by evacuation. The transportation director remained in the bus garage to coordinate additional efforts, including the calling up of additional drivers if needed.

SCT members who were pupil personnel specialists were asked to report to the administrative office for assignments. Essentially, their immediate task was to address the psychological complications of the crisis victims. Their more long-range task was designing mental health intervention strategies, including intensive individual attention for small or large groups of students.

As prearranged, the community mental health department's crisis team was also called to assemble at the SCT room. The group assisted in the psychological management of the crisis and helped in planning such matters as communication of death information to media team members.

The media team was briefed by this group in the SCT room. Because some members of the SCT were from the local media, most of the media personnel covering the incident were already sensitized to the complex issues surrounding coverage of a suicide, particularly that of an adolescent.

As information became more available on the incident (after the arrival of paramedics, who verified the student's death and the severity of the assistant principal's wound), available SCT members conferred in the crisis-team room to determine exactly who was to be notified and how. According to the crisis plan, the SCT coordinators and team members quickly decided what information to release to parents and guardians so that there would be consistency in what was communicated. The parents or guardians of each child in the class where the shooting took place were called by SCT designates. They were told that their child, although perfectly safe, had witnessed a shooting at school. They were asked to pick up the child from school and were again reassured that their daughter or son was safe.

As prearranged, the students in the crisis-origin building who had not been involved were taken to the gymnasium, where they were given a brief statement about the events. The class who had witnessed the shooting was taken to a separate "safe area," where they awaited the arrival of the pupil personnel specialists and mental health workers, who were at that time en route. The debriefing of this class was confined to answering questions and providing insights into the tragedy. Some of the topics covered included why some people act irrationally under stress, how some events cannot be easily understood, and how important social support can be in times of crisis.

Meanwhile, parents had been arriving to pick up their children. As they arrived, they were taken to a different room in which they were also debriefed. Previously designated and trained PTA/PTO members were available to provide needed support. When both the parents' and the children's debriefing sessions were over, parents were allowed to take their children home.

The rest of the student body remained in the gymnasium for the remainder of the afternoon (in this case, only a brief time) and were dismissed at the regular hour. Designated teachers accompanied students on the buses as a precautionary measure. Parents who came to pick up their children were given as much information about the event as the SCT had determined would be disseminated.

That night, a meeting was held by the SCT members for the community to answer further questions, discuss the process of student adjustment, and provide the names and telephone numbers of mental health specialists that the students could work with if needed.

School was cancelled for the following day to give the students a chance to recover and the school staff time to address various urgent issues. Teachers held a meeting that morning to prepare for students' return and to give them the chance to express their own adjustment responses and concerns. They were coached in how to address their classes by an experienced SCT member, a community psychiatrist. They rehearsed how to answer basic questions and manage students' concerns.

The next day the SCT members with clinical experience made themselves available during school hours, talking with students and teachers on an as-needed basis. Toward the end of the school day, interested parents came to another debriefing session to discuss what had happened, how students were going to adjust, what parents should expect from their grieving children, and how they could arrange for aftercare.

Finally, the school administration announced plans for weekly support meetings for parents. These meetings would address not only anticipatory guidance measures for parents but also adolescent stress, depression, and the grief and mourning process. Prevention and intervention strategies for adolescent suicide would also be discussed.

SUMMARY

The purpose of the SCT is to manage and control any crisis event that affects members of the school system. In developing the SCT, the first steps are to determine the group's purpose and personnel. Crisis team personnel must be selected to maximize the SCT's effectiveness. Toward this end, personnel should be included from the following groups:

the school system (including the superintendent, principals, faculty, support staff, and pupil personnel staff) and the community (e.g., emergency personnel, physicians and psychologists, social workers, city administrators, the media, and PTA/PTO representatives).

Because grief and mourning are the inevitable results of a tragedy, the SCT should be prepared to assist mourners with the grief and mourning process. This process also has implications for the development of the SCT program.

Responsibilities of the SCT generally include prevention efforts, efficient and effective intervention in suicide attempts and completions, and responsible postvention. The team can serve as an organizing body to provide training and education for students and faculty who will serve in these efforts.

In the unfortunate case that a crisis cannot be averted, it is the SCT's responsibility to make sure that the physical and psychological harm to everyone involved is minimal; that the necessary steps to end the crisis are taken; that law enforcement officials, medical personnel, and parents or guardians are informed; that an information network to dispel rumors and inform concerned parties is set up; and that the media treat the incident responsibly.

In addition, the SCT, school administration, and school staff and faculty must have postvention plans ready to implement. From planning a memorial service to providing mourners with therapy, referral, and peer counseling opportunities, the school system should always have a comprehensive postvention plan in place. The SCT may also find that follow-up efforts involving the community can help prevent future adolescent suicides. Finally, to prevent potential cluster suicides, both school and community mental health resources must monitor and intervene with youths identified as being at risk in the aftermath of a completed suicide.

CHAPTER 6

Suicide Issues With Special Populations

The preceding five chapters have offered a general perspective of adolescent suicide and prevention, intervention, and postvention techniques. Although gender and geographical location have been discussed in chapter 1 as they relate to the problem of youth suicide, other demographic considerations play an increasingly important role in adolescent suicide. This chapter will detail certain trends and dynamics of the suicide problem among the following groups: Native American, African American, and Hispanic American populations; lesbian and gay youth; youth with eating disorders; and college students.

With the exception of college students, members of these groups struggle not only with the typical conflicts of adolescence but also with the added burdens of discrimination, alienation, and disenfranchisement. An examination of the literature that exists on all these groups suggests that specific strategies for intervention may be necessary.

In particular, this chapter provides some insights into the demographics, presumed causal factors, and psychosocial treatment issues relating to these groups. Specific treatment considerations for each group will also be discussed. With the exception of the section on youth with eating disorders, in which females are overrepresented, the focus is primarily on adolescent males because they are most at risk.

SUICIDE AMONG RACIAL MINORITIES
IN THE UNITED STATES

The ability to develop a functional identity within the context of a society is directly associated with family and cultural legacies. Native American, African American, and Hispanic American adolescents live in a dual world. Seiden (1971) suggests that the more pluralistic our culture becomes, the greater the breakdown of subcultural mores. As traditions and social relationships deteriorate, the greater the suicidal vulnerability among members of the subculture.

As cultural assimilation occurs in the Hispanic community, for example, the remnants of Mexican, Puerto Rican, and Cuban cultural traditions diminish. This may create cultural confusion for Hispanic American youth. Unable to integrate into their new context but no longer firmly rooted in their own cultural and social traditions, such youths exist in a type of "nowhere land" where the search for identity may be overwhelming.

Many ethnic groups have embraced the notion of rediscovering and actively perpetuating the traditions, achievements, and values of their cultures. Although minority youth gain ethnic knowledge and pride from this endeavor, they must simultaneously attempt to assimilate into the mainstream culture. It is not difficult to imagine the anger and frustration of minority youths torn by the contrast between their own and the mainstream culture, and by the fact that the mainstream culture rejects and devalues their culture. Consider, for example, these reflections of an African American graduate student:

> I felt like I had some sense of belonging until I went to college. My background of learning, playing, and just developing in an all-black environment didn't at all prepare me for the experience of attending a college where white values, customs, and traditions were pervasive. The first years were the most difficult of my life. I made it in spite of anger and rejection. But most of my black classmates didn't.

When the minority youth experiences the broader culture as rejecting, this rejection blocks the formation of his or her identity. Unfortunately, the burden of adjustment falls on the youth, who must either learn to negotiate two worlds or fall victim to the mainstream culture's indifference.

Suicide Rates

Among racial and ethnic minorities in the United States for whom data exists on suicide rates—such as Native Americans (Dizmang, Watson, May, & Bopp, 1974; Tonkin, 1984), African Americans (Davis, 1985; Gibbs, 1988), and Hispanic Americans (Smith, Mercy, & Rosenberg, 1989)—younger adolescent males seem to commit suicide significantly more often than do their female counterparts. Figure 6.1 offers a graphic comparison of male and female suicide rates among white and nonwhite adolescents.

As shown in Figure 6.1, suicide rates among youth are higher for males and whites than for females and nonwhites. This trend has remained relatively constant over the last 30 years. However, suicide rates among nonwhite males have steadily risen during that same time

Figure 6.1   Suicide Rate by Gender for 15–19-Year-Old Whites and Nonwhites (1960–1988)

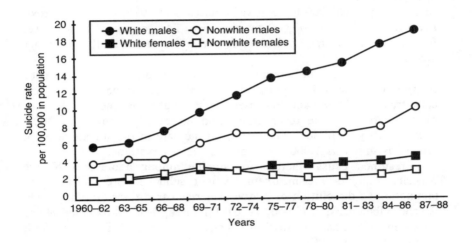

Note. From *Vital Statistics of the United States: Vol. 2. Mortality—Part A* (pp. 9–10) by the National Center for Health Statistics, 1992. Washington, DC: U. S. Government Printing Office.

period, with a particularly dramatic increase among Hispanic and Native American adolescent males (Berlin, 1987; Smith et al., 1989; Thompson, 1989).

A more dramatic finding regarding studies focusing on rates of suicide among various ethnic groups is that suicide rates for African American, Native American, and Hispanic American males peak in the adolescent and young adult years. After age 34, suicide rates drop off sharply for Native Americans and Hispanic Americans (Smith et al., 1989; Thompson, 1989). For white males, however, suicide rates continue to increase with age. African American male suicide rates remain relatively constant after tapering off in the middle adult years (Baker, 1989).

Native American Youth

Native American youth are reportedly the minority group with the highest rates of suicide. Adolescent males within the group are at particular risk (Garland & Zigler, 1993). The vulnerability of Native Americans to violent death, substance abuse, and suicide has been well documented (Berlin, 1987). As for African American and Hispanic American males, the suicide rate for Native American males is particularly marked during adolescence and the young adult years (Berlin, 1987; Berman & Jobes, 1991). McIntosh (1984) documented a suicide rate of 31 per 100,000 for Native Americans in 1976, with an approximate rate of 71 per 100,000 for the 15 to 24 age group. This is over four times the average suicide rate for white males in the same age group.

Suicide attempt and completion rates vary considerably from tribe to tribe and tend to be higher where tribal relocation has been historically frequent. Hafen and Frandsen (1986) found that the suicide completion rate on some reservations had increased as much as 300% during a 20-year period. The estimated increase in the suicide attempt rate is as much as 1,000% on those same reservations.

Presumed causal factors for suicide among adolescent Native Americans include racism, unemployment, school failure, and the contamination or dissolution of Native American traditions (Jordan, 1988; Wyche, Obolensky, & Glood, 1990). Of these, drug and alcohol abuse are often ranked as most critical (Beauvais, Oetting, & Edwards, 1985; Berman & Jobes, 1991).

African American Youth

Although rates of African American adolescent suicide have consistently been lower than those for white youth, suicide rates among adolescent African American males nearly tripled between the 1960s and late 1980s (Earls & Jemison, 1986; National Center for Health Statistics, 1989).

Despite the fact that African American females have the lowest rate of suicide among any ethnic group, there has still been a reported increase of 33% in this group over the last 40 years (Baker, 1989). During this same time period, suicide rates for adolescent white females have steadily increased. No study to date seems to explain the difference in suicide rates between African American males and females or between African American females and their white counterparts.

Hispanic American Youth

Not much is known about suicide among Hispanic Americans (Smith et al., 1989). As among the white population, the peak period for Hispanic American suicide appears to be during the adolescent and young adult years. Proportionately, however, significantly more suicides are reported among young Hispanics than among young Anglos (Smith et al., 1989). Smith et al. (1989) found that over 30% of Hispanic suicides were within the 15 to 24 age group, versus 16% for white adolescents. The data thus suggest that suicide is a major threat to Hispanic youth. Jobes, Berman, and Josselman (1986) hypothesize that current figures on rates of Hispanic American suicide are inaccurate in part due to inconsistencies in documenting and reporting suicide among the Hispanic population. However, as Hispanic American males grow older, their rates of suicide drop sharply, particularly in comparison to white males (Centers for Disease Control, 1992).

In addition, approximately 60% of all Hispanic Americans reside in the rural Southwest, a region with unusually high rates of suicide (Smith et al., 1989). The suicide rate for whites in these states is nearly 25% higher than for whites nationally. (See chapter 1 for discussion of rural versus urban suicide rates.)

Sociocultural Vulnerability

Suicide among adolescent minority groups may be explained in part by considerations unique to their minority status. Specifically, these concern social disenfranchisement, family dissolution, poverty, and school failure.

Social disenfranchisement. As noted previously, when minority adolescents aspire to enter the mainstream in a competitive society they pay a heavy price, many times facing discrimination, frustration, and failure.

Family dissolution. A traditional buffer for minorities living in a hostile or unreceptive society has been ethnic cohesion. In the past, minority families stuck together—they had to. However, as the family continues to disintegrate and communities no longer function as extended families, the minority youth is left without valuable sources of support, acceptance, and encouragement.

Poverty. Another obvious precipitant of depression, hopelessness, and helplessness in minority youth is the fact that many are growing up in impoverished conditions. About one-half of African American, Hispanic American, and Native American people live in or near poverty (Zaslow & Takanishi, 1993).

Besides contributing to malnutrition, poor housing, and inadequate health care, poverty is also directly correlated with crime. Homicide is the second leading cause of death among both children and adolescents across all ethnic groups, with African American males being particularly vulnerable (Hammond & Yung, 1993). The likelihood of being the victim of violence is two to four times greater for all minority groups than for their white counterparts (Dryfoos, 1990; Hammond & Yung, 1993; Indian Health Service, 1990; Smith et al., 1986).

It is easy to see why a minority youth surrounded by hunger, desperation, and violence—and who regularly encounters the mainstream's racism and indifference—may feel hopeless about finding a way up and out of his or her present situation.

School failure. Success in the educational system has traditionally been viewed as a way of ensuring one's future prosperity. However, between the growing discrepancy in the quality of schools and the rates at which minority youth are either failing or dropping out of schools, education is no longer a viable means for many of these youths to improve their standard of living. School failure results in a bind for minority students that tends to keep them trapped in poverty. African American and Hispanic American youth are twice as likely to drop out of school than their white counterparts (Bock & Moore, 1986), and it is equally unlikely that they will find employment when they do so (Rotherman-Borus, Rosario, & Koopman, 1991).

The failure of minority youth in the school system can be traced to numerous socioeconomic factors that have no bearing on their intelligence or abilities; unfortunately, the end result is simply that many minority youths feel trapped in a cycle of poverty from which there appears to be no escape.

Treatment Issues

Clinical issues relating to minority populations are essentially the same as for nonminority groups. However, one's minority status mandates unique approaches that address this variable.

Existential Concerns

Minority youth manifest specific existential concerns, primarily in the personal identity issues that are so often ambiguous during adolescence. The question "Who am I in relation to others?" is central for any adolescent, but when the young person is threatened by discrimination and isolation, the answer to such a question is particularly difficult.

On an individual level, treatment of existential concerns involves helping minority youths maintain respect for their cultural diversity, stand firm against suggestions that their ethnic differences imply inadequacy, and work to help others see that they, too, can succeed. One Hispanic American social worker remarked:

> It wasn't until I got past my anger at being Hispanic that
> I was able to look at myself, my family, and my Hispanic
> tradition objectively. Fortunately I had a counselor who was

sensitive to cultural issues (she was black) and helped me to get over the fury that I was carrying around. Eventually, I came to appreciate my background, and now I carry myself with pride. It's a particular joy to be able to help other minority students with that challenge. I guess part of the task is modeling my survivorship and my pride at the same time.

The challenge for society is to adopt community- and school-based prevention and intervention strategies that reflect cultural dynamics. Community-based mental health programs need to incorporate clinical interventions targeted toward their minority clientele. This will involve the employment of minority therapists to provide essential services and assist in the development of preventive outreach programs. The school curriculum should address the specific needs of minority students through coursework focusing on questions that minority adolescents pose to themselves regarding personal identity, racial integration, and social assimilation.

Prevention Tasks

In recommending specific prevention tasks for those intervening with Native American clients, James Thompson (1989) of the National Institute of Mental Health provides a framework that could be applied to all minority youth. His recommendations concern the following:

1. Improving socioeconomic conditions

2. Recognizing and treating underlying psychiatric disorders

3. Coordinating health services (including mental health and substance abuse services)

4. Addressing cultural conflicts among young people

Unless the social and economic conditions that predispose these young people to psychological and physical disorders are addressed and remediated, minority adolescents will continue to be at risk for suicide.

Specific Clinical Interventions

The following treatment modalities are effective with any group, but, as noted, may be particularly helpful with minority populations.

Family therapy. It is easy for a minority family to lose perspective when daily living presents ongoing conflicts and struggles that inhibit looking forward and planning meaningfully for the future. Family therapy can address not only specific family issues that contribute to adolescent depression but also issues of social integration that may affect the entire family (Pfeffer, 1981). When systems theory is incorporated into family interventions, it may help provide family members with a view of the family's position in society that they might not have developed previously (Goldenberg & Goldenberg, 1991; Oster & Caro, 1990; Richman, 1986).

Group treatment. Group treatment offers particular advantages because, in the group, disillusioned and disenfranchised minority youths can ventilate their mutual frustrations and obtain solace from one another. Support groups also offer depressed and suicidal minority adolescents the opportunity to relate to one another in an atmosphere of similarity in dysfunction. The therapeutic benefit of knowing another's plight when it is similar to your own can be remarkable, particularly when isolation and helplessness are a part of the clinical profile. A number of authors offer guidelines for and evidence of the productive outcomes of group counseling with suicidal minority adolescents (e.g., Edwards & Edwards, 1984; Franklin, 1982; Hendersen, 1979; McIntosh & Santos, 1984).

Cognitive-behavioral therapy. Cognitive-behavioral therapy has been demonstrated useful in alleviating negative thinking about the present and future (Beck, Rush, Shaw, & Emery, 1979). In brief, interventions based on this approach can be effective in altering the belief systems of minority adolescents, who tend to manifest negative and pessimistic thoughts and thought patterns.

Such thinking is epitomized in the comments of a now-successful Native American psychologist:

> When I looked around me and saw what the future held,
> I had no desire to go on ... if I would turn out like the
> guys who were doing drugs and booze, on the dole and
> looking for fights everywhere ... it just meant nothing. The
> future held nothing for me or anyone like me. Before my
> [suicide] attempt I just couldn't stop thinking bad things
> about me and my roots.

The cognitive distortions that accompany such depressive thinking can easily propel individuals toward self-destruction. It is important to point out, however, that when those thoughts are validated by impoverished social conditions, lack of opportunity, and institutionalized racism, they are difficult to refute.

The potency of such interventions are generally enhanced if the therapist is of the same ethnic background as the client. Thus, the Hispanic American psychotherapist offers a unique blend of insight, empathy, and skill to the Hispanic American adolescent who sees no hope for the future and is thus suicidal.

Peer counseling. Peer counseling is a strategy that has a multitude of advantages for minority youth. Because suicidal adolescents often turn to their peers with their problems, it is logical to identify, train, and supervise adolescents in the community and school settings to act as peer counselors. Peer counselors may then be trained to identify suicidal peers and to listen, respond therapeutically, and provide referral to counselors and professionals. Lenihan and Kirk (1990) have documented the effectiveness of working with peer counselors for students identified as being at risk for suicide.

Minority peer counselors could sensitize those working with minority groups to the issues surrounding adolescent suicide. The training of peer counselors to help identify such adolescents may also have a preventive effect. Community members, leaders, teachers, administrators, and peers become more aware not only of the problem of adolescent suicide but also of possible solutions. Thompson (1986) provides guidelines for developing such a program in the school and documents the multiple returns of such a therapeutic venture.

SUICIDE AMONG LESBIAN AND GAY YOUTH

Suicide Rates

Lesbian and gay youth have been found to be at inordinate risk for both suicide attempts and completions. This fact has been underscored recently by Gibson's (1989) report for the Secretary's Task Force on Youth Suicide, asserting that suicide is the leading cause of death among gay, lesbian, bisexual, and transsexual youth. Adolescents with alternative sexualities face family, peer, and social rejection, as well as personal confusion. Under such pressures, homosexual adolescents are two to six times more likely than their heterosexual counterparts to attempt suicide (Harry, 1989). The majority of such attempts occur among younger homosexual youths.

Treatment Issues

Risk Factors

The following risk factors are especially pertinent for this group.

Family factors. Often involved in adolescent suicide, family factors play a significant role in the problems of homosexual adolescents. As many as one-third of the lesbian and gay youths interviewed by the National Gay Task Force (1984) were noted to have been the victims of verbal abuse from relatives. The incidence of physical abuse and divorce in the family is also greater among homosexual youth (Gibson, 1989).

Self-esteem. Common enough among all adolescents, self-esteem problems are compounded in lesbian and gay youth. A lesbian college student recalls how she was made to feel about her sexuality when she opened up to a few people:

> When I sort of tested the waters and let some people know that I was gay I knew it would be tough, but I was not at all prepared for the onslaught of abuse and anger that occurred. It was tough enough trying to shield myself from my own confusion, but when everyone turned on me I wanted to die in the worst way possible. Maybe it was the suicide attempt that made everyone realize just how miserable I really was. I didn't like myself in the early days. It was horrible when everyone else also showed their dislike. I'm surprised I survived it.

The homosexual adolescent is in a quandary about sexual identity that confounds the development of self-esteem. "Coming out of the closet" is, in part, an effort to validate an already shaky identity. When that attempt is met with derision, disgust, moral outrage, and hostility—as it often is—the lesbian or gay youth will likely withdraw in confusion and feel even more isolated. Dysfunctional relationships, substance abuse, and depression are common among lesbian and gay youth and can easily increase suicidal risk.

The school environment. Typically, the adjustment problems of homosexual adolescents are compounded by the school environment. Hunter and Schaecher (1987) have documented the multiple stresses and crises faced by lesbian and gay youth in the school setting, including verbal and physical abuse.

Other causes of suicidal behavior among homosexual youth include conflicts with lovers (Bell & Weinberg, 1978), religious confusion (Gibson, 1989), and social isolation (Los Angeles Suicide Prevention Center, 1986; Tartagni, 1978).

Specific Counseling Concerns

In some cases, school professionals may find it easy to identify at-risk lesbian and gay youth because they are ostracized by their peers.

However, it is dangerous to rely on such opinions because, on the one hand, gossip is not always correct, and, on the other, many youths who are in conflict over their sexual identity remain quiet about it. Davis and Sandoval (1991) estimate that as many as 15% of students in junior and senior high schools are struggling with this intensely emotional issue. Such students typically don't publicize their struggles.

Prevention and intervention strategies should include both broad-based social measures and more specific clinical interventions for community and school counselors. The following are recommendations for helping the school and the community conduct appropriate identification and intervention with lesbian and gay students who are at risk for suicide.

Government or private sector awareness programs. Such programs could fund training for school and community practitioners and include clinical guidelines for the treatment of a youthful homosexual clientele. This would help to ensure a consistency of early identification and intervention. Within this context, it could become standard operating procedure for pupil personnel specialists, mental health practitioners, and health service providers to routinely include a suicide assessment as part of their ongoing work with lesbian and gay adolescents.

Support services for family members. Parents of lesbian and gay youths often describe themselves as victims and have concomitant adjustment issues that, if treated early, can defuse an already volatile family situation. Providing the family with outside support may help to prevent the trauma and conflict that drive some rejected youths away from home and into the streets.

Information about homosexuality. Curriculum-based offerings to provide appropriate information about homosexuality would help demystify the subject. Such information might help create a less hostile environment in which homosexual youths might stabilize and personally reorganize.

In addition to these efforts, educators and intervenors might need to reevaluate their attitudes about homosexuality. Even the most subtle prejudice can create grossly unjust personal, educational, and clinical iniquities for homosexual youth. If an intervenor is experiencing anxiety about working with a homosexual youth, consultation with a professional or clinical colleague—or a parent of a homosexual adolescent who has accepted the child's sexuality—might help reduce some of the dissonance.

SUICIDE AMONG YOUTH WITH EATING DISORDERS

Eating disorders are generally of two types: *Anorexia nervosa's* distinguishing feature is that individuals suffering from it will literally starve themselves to death while maintaining all the while that they are overweight. Anorexics suffer from an intense fear of obesity. In addition, female anorexics will generally have missed at least three consecutive menstrual periods. The dangers of anorexia go beyond the vulnerability it creates for suicide: Anorexia alone produces a mortality rate of between 5 and 18% (American Psychiatric Association, 1987; Szmukler & Russell, 1986).

Bulimia, on the other hand, is characterized by intermittent episodes of binging followed by some type of purging. Vomiting is a common method of purging, but many young women abuse laxatives and diuretics for this purpose. Although generally at a normal weight, the bulimic typically has phobic fears about being fat and becomes obsessed with weight loss. A bulimic adolescent will demonstrate excessive concern with body shape and weight; abuse laxatives, diuretics, and exercise to stay thin; vomit to purge after binging; and binge about twice a week for 3 months or more (American Psychiatric Association, 1987).

Both anorexia and bulimia are disorders that manifest themselves early in life. Onset of these disorders is usually from early adolescence (i.e., around 12) to approximately age 25, although onset has been observed as early as age 9 and as late as age 35 (American Psychiatric Association, 1987). Foreyt (1986) estimates that the number of young women in the United States with eating disorders is as high as 15%. Females are so overrepresented that both anorexia and bulimia are considered disorders of gender, but approximately 5% of victims are male (Levine, 1988).

Suicide Rates

To date there are no reported studies in the United States focusing specifically on suicide completions in persons with eating disorders. Adolescents with eating disorders are, however, seen as being at high risk for suicide (Garland & Zigler, 1993).

Eating disorders put an adolescent's psychological balance and physiological well being in serious jeopardy. Depression is often a correlate of eating disorders, and thus anorexic and bulimic youth are especially vulnerable to suicide (Fairburn, 1985; Kandel, Raveis, & Davies, 1991). Some observers consider the eating disorders themselves to have self-destructive characteristics and to be a prolonged form of suicide (Garland & Zigler, 1993). This view is difficult to deny, inasmuch as the integrated traits of impulsiveness and destructiveness in many eating disorder victims seem to create an unusual vulnerability (Chiles, 1986). Eating disorders have also been found to be quite prevalent (62%) in a sample of women diagnosed as self-mutilators, itself a self-destructive clinical trait (Favazza & Conterio, 1989).

Treatment Issues

Social Influences

Why do so many adolescents, females in particular, suffer from eating disorders? The general consensus is that women face intense social pressure to conform to a particular standard of beauty. Not only are they labeled desirable or not based on how closely they match this standard, their intelligence and potential for success are also judged by their physical appearance. Unfortunately, the standard against which they are judged is neither achievable nor necessarily (from a health perspective) desirable for most. Normal adolescent self-doubts combined with this pervasive social message about body and self can be overwhelming.

The compulsion to avoid food or to binge and purge becomes such an entrenched pattern that the adolescent loses control and experiences a major interruption in psychosocial development. As peers journey through the typical tribulations of adolescence, the adolescent with an eating disorder begins to withdraw from crucial interactions. The disorder causes young people to feel shame and discouragement. These negative emotions often lead to feelings of helplessness and depression, and, eventually, the stage for suicide is set.

Assessment and Treatment Priorities

It is important to remain alert to the possibility of suicidal ideation and suicidal behavior in an adolescent with an eating disorder. Certain assessment and treatment priorities exist.

Medical intervention. Obtaining medical intervention is critical because of the physical complications that can occur in even a moderately advanced case of anorexia or bulimia (e.g., cessation of menstruation, electrolyte imbalance, nutritional deficiencies). When referral is made to a physician, it is imperative that the individual referring the adolescent detail the behaviors that relate specifically to the eating disorder. In addition, any symptoms related to suicidal behavior that accompany the disorder (e.g., depression, hopelessness, despair) also need to be communicated to the physician. A request that the physician assess the mental status of the adolescent should be made.

Consultation with parents. Consulting with the parents of an adolescent with an eating disorder is a delicate matter. If the eating disorder has been identified by an educator (i.e., school counselor, social worker, teacher), confidentiality must be a priority. The school may have specific guidelines about notification because the condition is a medical one and a health risk is present. Some type of preparation for consultation with parents is advisable, particularly if the intervenor senses that the parents are unaware of their child's disorder.

Complications often arise with parents who wish to avoid psychological treatment and who try to force their child to regain weight by policing eating. This type of parental response can quickly increase the youth's resistance and perhaps denial. School personnel should continue to monitor the student's progress for as long as needed and intervene again if necessary.

School and community programs. Widespread ignorance about eating disorders exists. As a 19-year-old student with bulimia once commented:

> If only I had known that what I was doing was wrong. If
> only someone had told me that my purging was going to
> lead me on such an incredible journey into pain and misery,
> I really think early on I would have listened. Maybe not, I
> don't really know, but there was nobody saying anything
> about bulimia ... nobody. How was I to know?

Students should be educated about the dynamics of all dangerous behavioral practices (e.g., substance abuse, unsafe sexual practices, eating disorders). In this way, they will be able to recognize these risky behaviors in their peers. Similarly, community programs will help families monitor their children's eating habits.

Education can be a key to prevention. If we can sensitize our youth to the unrealistic nature of the models presented to them and work to change the emphasis in our society from thin to healthy, we can reduce adolescent vulnerability and perhaps decrease premature deaths attributable to eating disorders.

SUICIDE AMONG COLLEGE STUDENTS

When most college students begin their academic journey, it is their first long-term separation from their family and friends. This change is often perceived as a loss of support, which creates a vulnerability that can lead to the development of suicidal ideation. This is particularly true in adolescents attending large universities (Carson et al., 1988; Peck & Schrut, 1971).

Suicide Rates

Reports of suicide attempts and completions among college students are variable. Schwartz and Reifler (1980) found a suicide rate of 7 per 100,000 students in 53 colleges and universities in the United States, which is well below the overall suicide rate in the 15 to 24 age bracket. However, Mishara (1982) suggested that college students seemed to be at higher risk for suicide when compared to similar groups of young people who had not gone to college. In an abbreviated review of college student suicide, Carson et al. (1988) estimate that 10,000 college students attempt suicide each year, with approximately 1,000 succeeding. More recent data suggest that suicidal ideation is common among college students (54%), with that same sample of students reporting a 10.3% suicide attempt rate (Meehan, Lamb, Saltzman, & O'Carroll, 1992). Considering the large numbers of college students experiencing depression as well as suicidal ideation (Carson & Johnson, 1985; Craig & Senter, 1972; Kirk & Davidson, 1989), suicide potential among this group remains a concern for health providers and parents.

Sources of Stress in College Students

The transition from a familiar and secure environment with parents or guardians to a college environment is often jarring. First-year undergraduate and graduate students are particularly vulnerable because of their recent relocation. They suddenly find themselves in a crowded, impersonal, and unfamiliar milieu. As a result, they are often anxious and fearful about the forthcoming challenges.

Overall, the loss of the previously established support system is a significant causal factor in college students' depression and suicidal ideation (Arnstein, 1986; Berkovitz, 1985). The loss of familiar friends, haunts, and family—even the old school and teachers—can result in the need for significant adjustment. At this time, previously undefined dependency needs may come to the forefront, and, if unmet, may foster feelings of loneliness and isolation, which in turn lead to feelings of depression and hopelessness.

Specific factors associated with suicide in this group concern interpersonal issues, academic pressure, and family issues.

Interpersonal issues. Interpersonal issues such as relationship break-ups or the failure to establish close interpersonal bonds tend to be the most common precipitating factors in college student suicides (Dashef, 1984; Hersh, 1985).

Academic pressure. A great source of stress for the college student is the pressure to achieve academic success. Usually, the student is competing with highly intelligent, motivated, and ambitious peers in a situation very unlike high school. Far from home, intimidated, and burdened by expectations from self, friends, and family, the college student may find that no matter how hard he or she works, success is not as easy as it was in high school. Because the college neophyte perceives the new environment as cold and impersonal, he or she feels unable to cope with the new stresses and requirements of the situation. Some students actually set the scene for failure through their inability to use appropriate study skills.

Family issues. As it does in the suicidal behavior of other adolescents, parental death, divorce, separation, or even relocation can jeopardize an already precarious psychological balance with a college student who is trying desperately to deal with the challenges of autonomy and freedom. In what is still considered ground-breaking work, Paffenbarger and Asnes (1966) analyzed the comprehensive records of over 40,000 students at two prestigious Eastern universities. The students in this sample who completed suicide were twice as likely to come from families where major illness, paternal death, or divorce had occurred. (Interestingly, death of a mother was not correlated with suicidal behavior.)

Treatment Issues

In a 20-year study of student suicides on one college campus in the Northeast, Kraft (1980) found that both depression and anxiety were clinical components of the presuicidal profile. Ironically and tragically, the majority of the students who took their lives had made contact with the counseling service at the university prior to their deaths. About 40% of them had made contact within a week of the suicide.

Screening new students seems an ideal strategy to identify and intervene with those at risk. Many institutions of higher education require freshmen to live in university owned or approved housing and dormitories. This does provide some opportunity to observe students outside of class. It is important to remember, however, that administrative intrusion into the lives of students must be both reasonable and justifiable. The following considerations and guidelines are offered to provide a comprehensive approach to prevention and intervention with suicidal college students.

Residence halls. When students are required to live in university housing such as residence halls, the administration can provide training in suicide assessment and intervention to resident assistants or hall counselors. Training sessions with housing office personnel produce more sensitive and clinically adept resident assistants, who can detect and refer high-risk students. Training includes efforts to teach the symptom profiles of suicidal students, the causal factors that increase suicide risk, and microcounseling strategies to help develop therapeutic relationships. With this training, resident assistants or hall counselors can sensitively facilitate appropriate disclosures from students whom they suspect are troubled, then make referrals for professional assessment and intervention. Such training needs to be offered to personnel from all university-affiliated living units on campuses, including fraternities and sororities, where social pressures may abound.

University programs. Programs sponsored by the university can be designed to distribute information to students, staff, faculty, and administration. Such efforts can help sensitize the academic community to a wide array of psychological problems in youth. It is hoped that such programs will better enable the campus population to identify students who may be specifically at risk for depression and suicide.

The programs offered may take many forms: panel discussions sponsored by the counseling center, informational meetings, speaker bureaus, and colloquia regarding the problem; a college newspaper series highlighting the issue; programs during new student orientation emphasizing the stressors of student life; and faculty and staff workshops to teach diagnostic and referral skills. The list is as long as the willingness of the college administration to address the problem.

The university counseling center. Staff at a university counseling center typically employ individuals with multidisciplinary expertise. These professionals can serve the entire campus community by identifying students at risk for suicide and initiating intervention strategies with self-referred students. Counseling centers serve as a resource for the entire college and are thus in an ideal position to organize and direct prevention, intervention, and postvention activities. Consulting psychiatrists, counseling psychologists, and other helping professionals can serve as consultants to departments and units throughout the college community, offering training, intervention, and education. Such centers can also offer outreach programs and take suicide issues into a more public forum.

Academic units. Certain academic units—such as psychology, sociology, and health studies (medical departments)—may provide additional consultants and expertise in campuswide programming and organization. When interdepartmental cooperation exists, the entire college community is more likely to become involved, which in turn increases the impact of prevention efforts.

Peer counseling. Sponsored by the counseling center, peer counseling programs make it possible for individual students to assist in identification and referral efforts. Such programs should involve both a high level of training and a constant, expert level of supervision. Peer counselors can be assigned to clients already in treatment, serving as models or companion therapists during the formal treatment process, or they may help identify high-risk individuals. More generally, their presence in the college community may help to sensitize others to suicide issues.

SUMMARY

This chapter has focused on specific populations of adolescents and their particular vulnerabilities to suicide. Racial minority youth, lesbian and gay youth, adolescents with eating disorders, and college students face specific social, economic, and environmental pressures relating to depression and suicide. These pressures must be considered when formulating prevention, intervention, and postvention for these groups.

Suicide rates for various ethnic minority groups vary, but all may experience sociocultural vulnerability as a result of social disenfranchisement, family dissolution, poverty, and school failure. These factors can contribute to suicide attempts and completions.

Adolescents with alternative sexualities have extremely high suicide rates. Estimates indicate that they are two to six times more likely to attempt suicide than their heterosexual counterparts. Youth with eating disorders are also particularly vulnerable to suicide.

Although reports of suicide rates among college students are variable, fairly recent data suggest that suicidal ideation is common among college students. Considering the large numbers of college students who are apparently experiencing depression, suicide potential among this group is a source of concern.

The following general techniques have been found to be particularly effective when working with these populations: assigning intervenors from the same racial background (for racial minority youth), employing counselors and therapists trained in the specific issues and needs of these groups of adolescents, raising general awareness of the vulnerability of these groups, and increasing school and community programming to address issues these youths face and to design specific intervention techniques.

References

Abraham, Y. (1978). Patterns of communication and rejection in families of suicidal adolescents. *Dissertation Abstracts International, 38*(8), 4669A.

Adams, J. (1980). *Understanding and managing stress.* San Diego: University Associates.

Albert, N., & Beck, A. (1975). Incidence of depression in early adolescence: A preliminary study. *Journal of Youth and Adolescence, 4,* 301–307.

Aldridge, D., & Dallos, R. (1986). Distinguishing families where suicidal behavior is present from families where suicidal behavior is absent. *Journal of Family Therapy, 8,* 243–252.

Allen, B. (1987). Youth suicide. *Adolescence, 22,* 271–290.

American Psychiatric Association. (1987). *Diagnostic and statistical manual of mental disorders* (3rd ed. rev.). Washington, DC: Author.

Anthony, E. J. (1975). Childhood depression. In E. J. Anthony & T. Benedek (Eds.), *Depression and human existence.* Boston: Little-Brown.

Arnstein, R. (1986). The place of college health services in the prevention of suicide and affective disorders. In G. Klerman (Ed.), *Suicide and depression among adolescents and young adults.* Washington, DC: American Psychiatric Press.

Baker, F. (1989). Black youth suicide. In *Report of the Secretary's Task Force on Youth Suicide: Vol. 3. Prevention and intervention in youth suicide* (DHHS Publication No. ADM 89–1623). Washington, DC: U. S. Government Printing Office.

Baldwin, B. (1978). A paradigm for the classification of emotional crises: Implications for crisis intervention. *American Journal of Orthopsychiatry, 48,* 538–551.

Barlow, C. (1984). *Headaches and migraine in childhood.* Philadelphia: Lippincott.

Barrett, T. (1985). *Youth in crisis: Seeking solutions to self-destructive behavior.* Longmont, CO: Sporis West.

Beauvais, F., Oetting, E. R., & Edwards, R. (1985). Trends in the use of inhalants among American Indian adolescents. *White Cloud Journal, 3*(4), 3–11.

Beck, A. T., Rush, A., Shaw, B., & Emery, G. (1979). *Cognitive therapy for depression.* New York: Guilford.

Beck, A. T., Ward, C., Mendelson, M., Mock, J., & Erbaugh, J. (1961). An inventory for measuring depression. *Archives of General Psychiatry, 4,* 561–571.

Bell, A., & Weinberg, M. (1978). *Homosexualities: A study of diversity among men and women.* New York: Simon and Schuster.

Berkovitz, I. (1985). The adolescent, schools, and schooling. *Adolescent Psychiatry, 12,* 162–176.

Berlin, I. N. (1987). Suicide among American Indian adolescents: An overview. *Suicide and Life-Threatening Behavior, 17,* 218–232.

Berman, A. L. (1988). Fictional depiction of suicide in television films and imitation effects. *American Journal of Psychiatry, 145,* 982–986.

Berman, A. L. (1989). Mass media and youth suicide prevention. In *Report of the Secretary's Task Force on Youth Suicide: Vol. 3. Prevention and interventions in youth suicide* (DHHS Publication No. ADM 89–1623). Washington, DC: U. S. Government Printing Office.

Berman, A. L., & Carroll, T. A. (1984). Adolescent suicide: A critical review. *Death Education, 8,* 53–64.

Berman, A. L., & Jobes, D. (1991). *Adolescent suicide: Assessment and intervention.* Washington, DC: American Psychological Association.

Bock, R., & Moore, E. (1986). *Advantage and disadvantage: A profile of American youth.* Hillsdale, NJ: Erlbaum.

Bowen, M. (1960). A family concept of schizophrenia. In D. Jackson (Ed.), *The etiology of schizophrenia.* New York: Basic.

Boyd, J. H. (1983). The increasing rate of suicide by firearms. *New England Journal of Medicine, 308,* 872–874.

Brent, D., Perper, J., Goldstein, C., Kolko, D., Allan, M., Allman, C., & Zelenak, T. (1988). Risk factors for adolescent suicide. *Archives of General Psychiatry, 45,* 581–588.

Brewer, T., & Faitak, M. (1989). Ethical guidelines for inpatient psychiatric care of children. *Professional Psychology: Research and Practice, 20,* 142–147.

Bumpass, L. L. (1984). Children and marital disruption: A replication and update. *Demography, 21,* 71–82.

Capuzzi, D. (1986). Intervention strategies for youth at risk. In A. McEvoy (Chair), *Suicide prevention in the schools.* Symposium sponsored by Learning Publications, Orlando, FL.

Carlson, G., & Cantwell, D. (1982). Suicidal behavior and depression in children and adolescents. *Journal of the American Academy of Pediatrics, 21,* 361–368.

Carson, N., & Johnson, R. (1985). Suicidal thoughts and problem-solving preparation among college students. *Journal of College Student Personnel, 26,* 484–487.

Carson, R. C., Butcher, J., & Coleman, J. (1988). *Abnormal psychology and modern life* (8th ed.). Glenview, IL: Scott, Foresman.

Centers for Disease Control. (1985). *Suicide surveillance report. Summary: 1970–1980.* Atlanta: U. S. Department of Health and Human Services, Public Health Service.

Centers for Disease Control. (1986). *Youth suicide in the United States, 1970–1980.* Atlanta: U. S. Department of Health and Human Services, Public Health Service.

Centers for Disease Control. (1991). *Morbidity and Mortality Weekly Report, 39*(13).

Centers for Disease Control. (1992). *Monthly vital statistics report: Final data.* Atlanta: U. S. Department of Health and Human Services, Public Health Service.

Chiles, J. (1986). *Teenage depression and suicide.* New York: Chelsea House.

Cohen-Sandler, R., & Berman, A. L. (1982). Life stress and symptomatology: Determinants of suicidal behavior in children. *Journal of the American Academy of Child Psychiatry, 21,* 178–186.

Cohen-Sandler, R., Berman, A. L., & King, R. (1982). A follow-up study of hospitalized suicidal children. *Journal of the American Academy of Child Psychiatry, 21,* 398–403.

Costello, E., & Angold, A. (1988). Scales to assess child and adolescent depression: Checklists, screens, and nets. *Journal of the American Academy of Child and Adolescent Psychiatry, 27,* 726–737.

Craig, L., & Senter, R. (1972). Student thoughts about suicide. *Psychological Record, 22,* 355–358.

Crumley, F. (1982). The adolescent suicide attempt: A cardinal symptom of a serious psychiatric disorder. *American Journal of Psychotherapy, 36*(2), 158–165.

Cull, J. G., & Gill, W. S. (1982). *Suicide Probability Scale.* Los Angeles: Western Psychological Services.

Curran, D. (1987). *Adolescent suicide behavior.* New York: Hemisphere.

D'Arcy, C., & Siddique, C. (1984). Psychological distress among Canadian adolescents. *Psychological Medicine, 14,* 615–625.

Dashef, S. (1984). Active suicide intervention by a campus mental health service: Operation and rationale. *Journal of American College Health, 33,* 118–122.

Davidson, L., & Gould, M. S. (1989). Contagion as a risk factor for youth suicide. In *Report of the Secretary's Task Force on Youth Suicide: Vol. 2. Risk factors for youth suicide* (DHHS Publication No. ADM 89-1622). Washington, DC: U. S. Government Printing Office.

Davis, J. (1985). Suicidal crises in schools. *School Psychology Review, 14,* 313–324.

Davis, J., & Sandoval, J. (1991). *Suicidal youth: School-based intervention and prevention.* San Francisco: Jossey-Bass.

Davis, J., Sandoval, J., & Wilson, M. (1988). Primary prevention of adolescent suicide. *School Psychology Review, 17,* 559–569.

Davis, R. (1979). Black suicide in the seventies: Current trends. *Suicide and Life-Threatening Behavior, 9,* 131–140.

Deykin, E., Alpert, J., & McNamara, J. (1985). A pilot study of the effect of exposure to child abuse or neglect on adolescent suicidal behavior. *American Journal of Psychiatry, 142,* 1299–1303.

Dizmang, L., Watson, J., May, P., & Bopp, J. (1974). Adolescent suicide at an Indian reservation. *American Journal of Orthopsychiatry, 44,* 43–49.

Dornbusch, S., Mont-Reynaud, R., Ritter, P., Chen, Z., & Steinberg, L. (1991). Stressful events and their correlates among adolescents of diverse backgrounds. In M. Colton & S. Gore (Eds.), *Adolescent stress: Causes and consequences.* New York: Aldine de Gruyter.

Doweiko, H. E. (1990). *Concepts of chemical dependency.* Pacific Grove, CA: Brooks/Cole.

Dryfoos, J. (1990). *Adolescents at risk: Prevalence and prevention.* New York: Oxford University Press.

Earls, F., & Jemison, A. (1986). Suicidal behavior in American Blacks. In G. Klerman (Ed.), *Suicide and depression among adolescents and young adults.* Washington, DC: American Psychiatric Press.

Eaton, M., Peterson, M., & Davis, J. (1981). Psychological factors affecting physical conditions. In M. Eaton, M. Peterson, & J. Davis (Eds.), *Psychiatry.* Garden City, NY: Medical Examination Publishing.

Eddy, D., Wolpert, R., & Rosenberg, M. (1989). Estimating the effectiveness of interventions to prevent youth suicides: A report to the Secretary's Task Force on Youth Suicide. In *Report of the Secretary's Task Force on Youth Suicide: Vol. 4. Strategies for the prevention of youth suicide* (DHHS Publication No. ADM 89–1624). Washington, DC: U. S. Government Printing Office.

Edwards, E. D., & Edwards, M. E. (1984). Group work practice with American Indians. *Social Work With Groups, 7*(3), 7–12.

Elkind, D. (1981). *The hurried child: Growing up too fast too soon.* Reading, MA: Addison-Wesley.

Elkind, D. (1984). *All grown up and no place to go: Teenagers in crisis.* Reading, MA: Addison-Wesley.

Ellis, A. (1970). Rational-emotive therapy. In L. Hersher (Ed.), *Four psychotherapies.* Norwalk, CT: Appleton-Century-Crofts.

Eyeman, J. (1987, March). *Suicide prevention in schools.* Preconference workshop presented at the annual meeting of the National Association of School Psychologists, New Orleans.

Fairburn, C. (1985). The management of bulimia nervosa. *Journal of Psychiatric Research, 19,* 465–472.

Farberow, N. L. (1989). Preparatory and prior suicidal behavior factors. In *Report of the Secretary's Task Force on Youth Suicide: Vol. 2. Risk factors for youth suicide* (DHHS Publication No. ADM 89–1622). Washington, DC: U. S. Government Printing Office.

Farberow, N. L., & Litman, R. (1970). *A comprehensive suicide prevention program: Suicide Prevention Center of Los Angeles, 1958–1969* (Unpublished Final Report). Washington, DC: Department of Health, Education and Welfare and the National Institute of Mental Health.

Favazza, A., & Conterio, K. (1989). Female habitual self-mutilators. *Acta Psychiatrica Scandinavica, 79,* 283–289.

Fencik, J. (Ed.). (1986). *A teacher's manual for the prevention of suicide among adolescents.* Providence, RI: Samaritans.

Foreyt, J. P. (1986). Treating the diseases of the 1980's: Eating disorders. *Contemporary Psychology, 31,* 313–332.

Franklin, A. J. (1982). Therapeutic interventions with urban black adolescents. In E. Jones & S. Korchin (Eds.), *Minority mental health.* New York: Praeger.

Frazier, S. H. (1989). Overview and recommendations. In *Report of the Secretary's Task Force on Youth Suicide: Vol. 1. Overview and recommendations* (DHHS Publication No. ADM 89–1621). Washington, DC: U. S. Government Printing Office.

Fritz, G. (1983). Childhood asthma. *Psychosomatics, 24,* 959–967.

Gallup, G. (1991). *The Gallup survey on teenage suicide.* Princeton, NJ: The George H. Gallup International Institute.

Garbarino, J., Sebes, J., & Schellenbach, C. (1984). Families at risk for destructive parent-child relations in adolescence. *Child Development, 55,* 174–183.

Garfinkel, B. D. (1989). School-based prevention programs. In *Report of the Secretary's Task Force on Youth Suicide: Vol. 3. Prevention and interventions in youth suicide* (DHHS Publication No. ADM 89–1623). Washington, DC: U. S. Government Printing Office.

Garfinkel, B. D., Froese, A., & Hood, J. (1982). Suicide attempts in children and adolescents. *American Journal of Psychiatry, 139,* 1257–1261.

Garland, A., & Zigler, E. (1993). Adolescent suicide prevention: Current research and social policy implications. *American Psychologist, 48,* 169–182.

Gibbs, J. (1988). Conceptual, methodological, and sociocultural issues in Black youth suicide: Implications for assessment and early intervention. *Suicide and Life-Threatening Behavior, 18,* 73–89.

Gibson, P. (1989). Gay male and lesbian youth suicide. In *Report of the Secretary's Task Force on Youth Suicide: Vol. 3. Prevention and interventions in youth suicide* (DHHS Publication No. ADM 89–1623). Washington, DC: U. S. Government Printing Office.

Gilliland, B., & James, R. (1988). *Crisis intervention strategies.* Pacific Grove, CA: Brooks/Cole.

Girdano, D., & Everly, G. (1979). *Controlling stress and tension: A holistic approach.* Englewood Cliffs, NJ: Prentice-Hall.

Goldenberg, I., & Goldenberg, H. (1991). *Family therapy: An overview.* Pacific Grove, CA: Brooks/Cole.

Gore, S., & Colten, M. (1991). Gender, stress, and distress: Social relational influences. In J. Eckenrode (Ed.), *The social context of stress and coping.* New York: Plenum.

Hafen, B. Q., & Frandsen, K. J. (1986). *Youth suicide: Depression and loneliness.* Evergreen, CO: Cordillera.

Hammond, W., & Yung, B. (1993). Psychology's role in the public health response to assaultive violence among young African American men. *American Psychologist, 48,* 142–154.

Harry, J. (1989). Sexual identity issues. In *Report of the Secretary's Task Force on Youth Suicide: Vol 2. Risk factors for youth suicide* (DHHS Publication No. ADM 89-1622). Washington, DC: U. S. Government Printing Office.

Hatton, C., & Valente, S. (1984). *Suicide assessment and intervention.* Norwalk, CT: Appleton-Century-Crofts.

Hawton, K. (1982). Annotation: Attempted suicide in children and adolescents. *Journal of Child Psychology and Psychiatry, 23,* 497–503.

Hawton, K. (1986). *Suicide and attempted suicide among children and adolescents.* Newbury Park, CA: Sage.

Hawton, K., O'Grady, J., Osborne, M., & Cole, D. (1982). Adolescents who take overdoses: Their characteristics, problems, and contacts with helping agencies. *British Journal of Psychiatry, 140,* 118–123.

Hendersen, G. (Ed.). (1979). *Understanding and counseling ethnic minorities.* Springfield: Charles C Thomas.

Hendren, R. L. (1990). Stress in adolescence. In L. E. Arnold (Ed.), *Childhood stress.* New York: Wiley.

Henker, F. (1984). Psychosomatic illness: Biochemical and physiologic foundations. *Psychosomatics, 25,* 19–24.

Hersh, J. B. (1985). Interviewing college students in crisis. *Journal of Counseling and Development, 61,* 286–289.

Hoberman, H. M., & Garfinkel, B. D. (1988). Completed suicide in children and adolescents. *Journal of the American Academy of Child and Adolescent Psychiatry, 27,* 689–695.

Hoelter, J. (1979). Religiosity, fear of death, and suicide acceptability. *Suicide and Life-Threatening Behavior, 9,* 163–172.

Holinger, P., & Offer, C. (1989). The prediction of adolescent suicide: A population model. *American Journal of Psychiatry, 139,* 302–307.

Holmes, T., & Rahe, R. (1967). The Social Readjustment Rating Scale. *Journal of Psychosomatic Research, 11,* 213–218.

Hunter, J., & Schaecher, R. (1987). Stress on lesbian and gay adolescents in schools. *Social Work in Education, 9,* 180–181.

Indian Health Service. (1990). *Injuries among American Indians and Alaskan Natives, 1990.* Rockville, MD: U. S. Public Health Service.

Ingersoll, G. (1989). *Adolescents*. Englewood Cliffs, NJ: Prentice-Hall.

Jacobs, J. J. (1971). *Adolescent suicide*. New York: Wiley.

Jacobson, A., & Leibovich, J. (1984). Psychological issues in diabetes mellitus. *Psychosomatics, 25,* 19–24.

Jobes, D., Berman, A. L., & Josselman, A. (1986). The impact of psychological autopsies on medical examiners' determination of manner of death. *Journal of Forensic Sciences, 31,* 170–189.

Johnson, S., & Maile, L. (1987). *Suicide and the schools*. Springfield, IL: Charles C Thomas.

Jordan, J. B. (1988). Interventions with Native Americans. In D. Capuzzi & L. Golden (Eds.), *Preventing adolescent suicide*. Muncie, IN: Accelerated Development.

Kandel, D., & Davies, M. (1982). Epidemiology of depressive mood in adolescents. *Archives of General Psychiatry, 39,* 1205–1212.

Kandel, D., Raveis, V., & Davies, M. (1991). The emergence of depressive symptoms during adolescence. *Journal of Youth and Adolescence, 20,* 289–309.

Kaplan, S., Hong, G., & Weinhold, C. (1984). Epidemiology of depressive symptomology in adolescents. *Journal of the American Academy of Child Psychiatry, 23,* 91–98.

Karolus, S., Kirk, W. G., & Shatz, M. (1990, February). *Identification of suicidal symptoms by high school students*. Paper presented at the annual meeting of the Illinois School Psychologists Association, Champaign, IL.

Kaslow, J. J., & Rehm, L. (1983). Child depression. In R. J. Morris & T. Kratochwill (Eds.), *The practice of child therapy*. Elmsford, NY: Pergamon.

Kerfoot, M. (1979). Self-poisoning by children and adolescents. *Social Work Today, 10,* 9–11.

Kessler, R., Downey, G., Milavsky, J., & Stipp, H. (1988). Clustering of teenage suicides after television news stories about suicides: A reconsideration. *American Journal of Psychiatry, 145,* 1379–1383.

Khan, A. (1987). Heterogeneity of suicidal adolescents. *Journal of the American Academy of Child and Adolescent Psychiatry, 26,* 92–96.

King, L., & Pittman, G. (1969). A six year follow-up of sixty-five adolescent patients: Predictive value of presenting clinical picture. *British Journal of Psychiatry, 115,* 1437–1441.

Kirk, W. G., & Davidson, K. (1989). *Influence of made-for-television movies about teen suicide on suicide acceptance and suicide vulnerability*. Unpublished manuscript, Eastern Illinois University, Charleston, IL.

Kirk, W. G., & Goecken, H. (1983, March). *Identification of suicide lethality factors*. Paper presented at the annual meeting of the Southeastern Psychological Association, Atlanta, GA.

Kirk, W. G., & Shatz, M. (1990, March). *Crisis management in the schools: Organization and implementation.* Paper presented at the annual meeting of the Illinois School Psychologists Association, Peoria, IL.

Kirk, W. G., & Walter, G. (1981). Support groups as a method to avoid burnout. *Education, 102,* 147–150.

Klerman, G., Weissman, M., & Rounsaville, E. (1984). *Interpersonal psychotherapy of depression.* New York: Basic.

Klingman, A., & Eli, Z. (1981). A school community in disaster: Primary and secondary prevention in situational crisis. *Professional Psychology, 12,* 523–533.

Kneisel, P., & Richards, G. (1988). Crisis intervention after the suicide of a teacher. *Professional Psychology, 19,* 165–169.

Kobasa, S. C. (1979). Stressful life events, personality, and health: An inquiry into hardiness. *Journal of Personality and Social Psychology, 37,* 1–11.

Kolko, D. J. (1987). Depression. In M. Hersen & V. B. Van Hasselt (Eds.), *Behavior therapy with children and adolescents: A clinical approach.* New York: Wiley.

Kosky, R., Silburn, S., & Zubrick, S. (1986). Symptomatic depression and suicidal ideation: A comparative study with children. *Journal of Nervous and Mental Disease, 174,* 523–528.

Kovacs, M., & Puig-Antich, J. (1989). Major psychiatric disorders as risk factors in youth suicide. In *Report of the Secretary's Task Force on Youth Suicide: Vol. 2. Risk factors for youth suicide* (DHHS Publication No. ADM 89–1622). Washington, DC: U. S. Government Printing Office.

Kraft, D. (1980). Student suicides during a twenty-year period at a state university campus. *Journal of the American College Health Association, 28,* 258–262.

Lamb, F., & Dunne-Maxim, K. (1987). Postvention in schools: Policy and process. In E. J. Dunne, J. L. McIntosh, & K. Dunne-Maxim (Eds.), *Suicide and its aftermath: Understanding and counseling the survivors.* New York: Norton.

Leder, M. (1987). *Dead serious: A book for teenagers about suicide.* New York: Atheneum.

Lenihan, G., & Kirk, W. G. (1990). Using student paraprofessionals in the treatment of eating disorders. *Journal of Counseling and Development, 68,* 332–335.

Levine, M. (1988, October). *Introduction to eating disorders: What the educator, health, and mental health professional needs to know.* Paper presented at the seventh annual National Conference on Eating Disorders of the National Anorexic Aid Society, Columbus, OH.

Lewinsohn, P., Garrison, C., Langhinrichsen, J., & Marsteller, F. (1989). *The assessment of suicidal behavior in adolescents: A review of scales suitable for epidemiologic and clinical research.* Rockville, MD: National Institute of Mental Health.

Los Angeles Suicide Prevention ·Center. (1986). *Problems of suicide among lesbian and gay adolescents.* Unpublished manuscript.

Luborsky, C., Singer, B., & Luborsky, L. (1975). Comparative studies of psychotherapies. *Archives of General Psychiatry, 32,* 995–1008.

Maher, B. (1970). *Psychopathology: A behavioral perspective.* New York: McGraw-Hill.

Matthews, K. (1981). Antecedents of the Type-A coronary-prone behavior pattern. In S. Brehn, S. Kassen, & F. Gibbons (Eds.), *Developmental social psychology.* New York: Oxford.

McBrien, J. (1983). Are you thinking of killing yourself? Confronting students' suicidal thoughts. *The School Counselor, 31*(1), 79–82.

McIntosh, J. L. (1984). Suicide among Native Americans: Further tribal data and considerations. *Omega, 14,* 215–229.

McIntosh, J. L., & Santos, J. (1984). Suicide counseling and intervention with racial/ethnic minorities. In C. Hatton & S. McBride-Valente (Eds.), *Suicide: Assessment and intervention* (2nd ed.). Norwalk, CT: Appleton-Century-Crofts.

McKenry, D., Tishler, C., & Kelley, C. (1982). Adolescent suicide: A comparison of attempters and non-attempters in an emergency room population. *Clinical Pediatrics, 21*(5), 266–270.

McKenry, D., Tishler, C., & Kelley, C. (1983). The role of drugs in adolescent suicide attempts. *Suicide and Life-Threatening Behavior, 13,* 166–175.

McWhirter, J., & Kigin, T. (1988). Depression. In D. Capuzzi & L. Golden (Eds.), *Preventing adolescent suicide.* Muncie, IN: Accelerated Development.

Meehan, P., Lamb, J., Saltzman, L., & O'Carroll, P. (1992). Attempted suicide among young adults: Progress toward a meaningful estimate of prevalence. *American Journal of Psychiatry, 149,* 41–44.

Mishara, B. (1982). College students' experiences with suicide and reactions to suicidal verbalizations: A model for prevention. *Journal of Community Psychology, 10,* 142–150.

Naisbitt, J. (1982). *Megatrends.* New York: Warner.

National Center for Health Statistics. (1989). *Monthly vital statistics report, 37*(13). Washington, DC: U. S. Government Printing Office.

National Center for Health Statistics. (1992). *Vital statistics of the United States: Vol. 2. Mortality—Part A.* Washington, DC: U. S. Government Printing Office.

National Center for Health Statistics. (1992). *Monthly vital statistics report: Final data, 40*(8). Washington, DC: U. S. Government Printing Office.

National Gay Task Force. (1984). *Anti-gay/lesbian victimization.* New York: Author.

National Institute of Mental Health. (1985). *Suicide in the United States: 1958-1982.* Washington, DC: U. S. Government Printing Office.

Nelson, E. R., & Slaikeu, K. A. (1984). Crisis intervention in the schools. In K. A. Slaikeu (Ed.), *Crisis intervention: A handbook for practice and research*. Boston: Allyn & Bacon.

Nottleman, E. D., Susman, D., Inoff-Germain, G., Cutler, G., Loriaux, D., & Chrousos, G. (1987). Developmental processes in early adolescence: Relationships between adolescent adjustment problems and chronological age, pubertal stage, and puberty related serum hormone level. *Journal of Pediatrics, 110*, 473–480.

Offer, D. (1969). *The psychological world of the teenager*. New York: Basic.

Ojanlatva, A., Hammer, A., & Mohr, M. (1987). The ultimate rejection: Helping the survivors of teen suicide victims. *Journal of School Health, 57*, 181–182.

Olson, D., McCubbin, H., Barnes, H., Larson, A., Muxen, M., & Wilson, M. (1983). *Families, what makes them work*. Newbury Park, CA: Sage.

Oster, G., & Caro, J. (1990). *Understanding and treating depressed adolescents and their families*. New York: Wiley.

Paffenbarger, R., & Asnes, D. (1966). Chronic disease in former college students: Precursors of suicide in early and middle life. *American Journal of Public Health, 56*, 1026–1036.

Patros, P. G., & Shamoo, T. (1989). *Depression and suicide in children and adolescents: Prevention, intervention and postvention*. Needham Heights, MA: Allyn & Bacon.

Paykel, E. S. (1982). *Handbook of affective disorders*. Edinburgh: Churchill Livingstone.

Pearlin, L., & Lieberman, M. (1979). Sources of emotional distress. *Resources in Mental Health, 1*, 217–248.

Peck, M. L. (1986). Completed suicides: Correlates of choice of method. *Omega, 16*, 309–323.

Peck, M. L., Farberow, N. L., & Litman, R. (1985). *Youth suicide*. New York: Springer.

Peck, M. L., & Schrut, A. (1971). Suicidal behavior among college students. *Health Sciences and Mental Health Administrators Health Reports, 86*(2), 149–156.

Petersen, A., Compas, B., Brooks-Gunn, J., Stemmler, M., Ey, S., & Grant, K. (1993). Depression in adolescence. *American Psychologist, 48*, 155–168.

Petersen, A., Sarigiani, P., & Kennedy, R. (1991). Adolescent depression: Why more girls? *Journal of Youth and Adolescence, 20*, 247–271.

Pfeffer, C. R. (1981). The family system of suicidal children. *American Journal of Psychotherapy, 35*, 330–341.

Pfeffer, C. R. (1986). *The suicidal child*. New York: Guilford.

Pfeffer, C. R., Conte, H. R., Plutchik, R., & Jerrett, I. (1980). Suicide behavior in latency-age children: An outpatient population. *Journal of the American Academy of Child and Adolescent Psychiatry, 19*, 703–710.

Phillips, D. P., & Carstensen, L. L. (1986). The clustering of teenage suicides after television news stories about suicide. *The New England
Journal of Medicine, 315,* 685–689.

Rando, T. A. (1984). *Grief, dying, and death: Clinical interventions for
caregivers.* Champaign, IL: Research Press.

Reich, T., Rice, J., & Mullaney, J. (1986). Genetic risk factors for the affective disorders. In G. Klerman (Ed.), *Suicide and depression among
adolescents and young adults.* Washington, DC: American Psychiatric
Press.

Reynolds, W. M. (1983, March). *Depression in adolescents: Measurement,
epidemiology, and correlates.* Paper presented at the annual meeting of
the National Association of School Psychologists, Detroit, MI.

Reynolds, W. M. (1987). *Suicidal Ideation Questionnaire.* Odessa, FL:
Psychological Assessment Resources.

Richman, J. (1984). The family therapy of suicidal adolescents: Promises
and pitfalls. In H. S. Sudak, A. Ford, & N. Rushforth (Eds.), *Suicide
in the young.* Boston: Wright.

Richman, J. (1986). *Family therapy for suicidal people.* New York: Springer.

Robbins, D., Alessi, N., Cook, S., Poznanski, E., & Yanchyshyn, G. (1982).
The use of diagnostic criteria (RDC) for depression in adolescent
psychiatric inpatients. *Journal of the American Academy of Child
Psychiatry, 2,* 251–255.

Robbins, D., & Kashani, J. (1986). Depression in adolescence. In D. Robbins
(Ed.), *Advances in adolescent mental health* (Vol. 1). Greenwich, CT:
Jason Aronson.

Rosenberg, M., Smith, J., Davidson, L., & Conn, J. (1987). The emergence
of youth suicide: An epidemiologic analysis and public health perspective. *Annual Reviews of Public Health, 8,* 417–440.

Rotherman-Borus, M., Rosario, M., & Koopman, C. (1991). Minority
youths at high risk. In M. Colten & S. Gore (Eds.), *Adolescent stress:
Causes and consequences.* New York: Aldine de Gruyter.

Rubenstein, J. L. (1989). Suicidal behavior in "normal" adolescents: Risk
and protective factors. *American Journal of Orthopsychiatry, 59,* 59–71.

Rutter, M., Graham, P., Chadwick, O., & Yule, W. (1976). Adolescent turmoil: Factor or fiction? *Journal of Child Psychology and Psychiatry,
17,* 35–56.

Schneider, J. (1984). *Stress, loss, and grief: Understanding their origins and
growth potential.* Baltimore: University Park Press.

Schuckit, M., & Schuckit, J. (1989). Substance use and abuse: A risk fac-
tor in youth suicide. In *Report of the Secretary's Task Force on Youth
Suicide: Vol. 2. Risk factors for youth suicide* (DHHS Publication No.
ADM 89–1622). Washington, DC: U. S. Government Printing Office.

Schwartz, A. J., & Reifler, C. G. (1980). Suicide among American college
and university students from 1970 through 1976. *Journal of the American College Health Association, 28,* 205–210.

Seiden, R. H. (1971). The problem of suicide on college campuses. *Journal of the American College Health Association, 41,* 243–248.

Seligman, M. E. (1975). *Helplessness: On depression, development, and death.* San Francisco: Freeman.

Selye, H. (1976). *The stress of life* (2nd ed.). New York: McGraw-Hill.

Shaffer, D., & Gould, M. (1987). *A study of completed and attempted suicide in adolescents* (Progress Report, Grant No. 38198). Rockville, MD: National Institute of Mental Health.

Shafii, M., Carrigan, S., Whittinghill, J. R., & Derrick, A. (1985). Psychological autopsy of completed suicide in children and adolescents. *American Journal of Psychiatry, 142,* 1061–1064.

Sheperd, M., Oppenheim, B., & Mitchell, S. (1971). *Childhood behavior and mental health.* New York: Grune and Stratton.

Simons, A., Murphy, G., Levine, J., & Wetzel, R. (1986). Cognitive therapy and pharmacology for depression: Sustained improvement over one year. *Archives of General Psychiatry, 43,* 43–48.

Sloan, J. H., Rivara, F. P., Reay, D. T., Ferris, J. A., & Kellerman, A. L. (1990). Firearm regulations and rates of suicides: A comparison of two metropolitan areas. *New England Journal of Medicine, 322,* 369–373.

Smetana, J., Yau, J., Restrepo, A., & Braeges, J. (1991). Conflict and adaptation in adolescence: Adolescent-parent conflict. In M. Colten & S. Gore (Eds.), *Adolescent stress: Causes and consequences.* New York: Aldine de Gruyter.

Smith, J. C., Mercy, J., & Rosenberg, M. (1986). Suicide and homicide among Hispanics in the Southwest. *Public Health Reports, 101,* 265–270.

Smith, J. C., Mercy, J., & Rosenberg, M. (1989). Hispanic suicide in the Southwest, 1980–1982. In *Report of the Secretary's Task Force on Youth Suicide: Vol. 3. Prevention and interventions in youth suicide* (DHHS Publication No. ADM 89–1623). Washington, DC: U. S. Government Printing Office.

Smith, K., & Crawford, S. (1986). Suicidal behavior among "normal" high school students. *Suicide and Life-Threatening Behavior, 16,* 313–325.

Strober, M., Green, J., & Carlson, G. (1981). Utility of the Beck Depression Inventory with psychiatrically hospitalized adolescents. *Journal of Consulting and Clinical Psychology, 49,* 482–483.

Suter, B. (1976). Suicide and women. In B. Wolman & H. Krauss (Eds.), *Between survival and suicide.* New York: Gardner.

Szmukler, G., & Russell, G. (1986). Outcome and prognosis of anorexia nervosa. In K. Brownell & J. Foreyt (Eds.), *Handbook of eating disorders.* New York: Basic.

Tartagni, D. (1978). Counseling gays in the school setting. *School Counselor, 26,* 26–32.

Thompson, J. (1989). Prevention of adolescent suicide among American Indian and Alaska Native peoples. In *Report of the Secretary's Task Force on Youth Suicide: Vol. 3. Prevention and interventions in youth suicide* (DHHS Publication No. ADM 89–1623). Washington, DC: U. S. Government Printing Office.

Thompson, R. (1986). Developing a peer group facilitation program on the secondary school level: An investment with multiple returns. *Small Group Behavior, 17,* 105–112.

Tonkin, R. S. (1984). Suicide methods in British Columbia. *Journal of Adolescent Health Care, 5,* 172–182.

Toolan, J. (1975). Suicide in children and adolescents. *American Journal of Psychotherapy, 29,* 339–344.

Topol, R., & Reznikoff, M. (1982). Perceived peer and family relationships: Hopelessness, locus of control as factors in adolescent suicide attempts. *Suicide and Life-Threatening Behavior, 12,* 141–150.

U. S. House of Representatives, Select Committee on Aging. (1985). *Suicide and suicide prevention* (Commission Publication No. 98–497). Washington, DC: U. S. Government Printing Office.

Walker, L., & Green, J. (1987). Negative life events, psychosocial resources and psychophysiological symptoms in adolescents. *Journal of Clinical Child Psychology, 16,* 29–36.

Wallerstein, J., & Kelly, J. (1980). *Surviving the breakup: How children and parents cope with divorce.* New York: Basic.

Wilkenson, K., & Israel, G. (1984). Suicide and rurality in urban society. *Suicide and Life-Threatening Behavior, 8,* 3–13.

Withers, L., & Kaplan, D. (1987). Adolescents who attempt suicide: A retrospective clinical chart review of hospitalized patients. *Professional Psychology: Research & Practice, 18,* 391–393.

Wyche, K., Obolensky, N., & Glood, E. (1990). American Indian, Black American, and Hispanic American youth. In M. J. Rotheram-Borus, J. Bradley, & N. Obolensky (Eds.), *Planning to live: Evaluating and treating suicidal teens in community settings.* Tulsa: University of Oklahoma Press.

Zaslow, M., & Takanishi, R. (1993). Priorities for research on adolescent development. *American Psychologist, 48,* 185–192.

Author Index

Subject Index

167

About the Author

William G. Kirk is a professor of psychology and coordinator of clinical graduate training at Eastern Illinois University, Charleston, Illinois. Dr. Kirk received his Ph.D. from the University of Kansas and is a licensed clinical psychologist and a certified school psychologist in the state of Illinois. In 1982–1983 Dr. Kirk served as a Courtesy Associate Professor of Psychology at the Center for Behavioral Medicine, University of South Florida, under the auspices of Dr. Charles Spielberger. More recently, he was a visiting professor of applied psychology at University College Cork, Cork, Ireland, where he taught in the graduate program and lectured in the medical college of the university. He has provided consultation services to schools, mental health agencies, hospitals, and industry throughout the Midwest. In addition, he has conducted workshops on loss, suicide, behavioral management, and eating disorders in Canada and Europe as well as in the United States.